A HISTORY OF MENSTON AND HAWKSWORTH

A HISTORY OF
MENSTON
AND
HAWKSWORTH

Alastair Laurence

Alastair Laurence

First published in 1991 by
Smith Settle Ltd
Ilkley Road
Otley
LS21 3JP

ISBN Paper 1 870071 75 1

Designed, printed and bound by
SMITH SETTLE
Ilkley Road, Otley, West Yorkshire LS21 3JP

CONTENTS

ACKNOWLEDGEMENTS

The author would like to thank the archivists of the West Yorkshire Archive Service for their assistance, in particular Maisie Morton and Sylvia Thomas. Thanks are also due to Anne Barker, Wendy Childs, John Cornwall and staff at Hawksworth Hall School, and Margery and Ramon Elias (USA).

The photographs of Hawksworth Hall and Menston Grange are reproduced by permission of the Royal Commission on the Historical Monuments of England. Simon Hawkesworth kindly provided the engraving of Sir Walter Hawksworth. The author thanks Nicholas and Susannah Horton-Fawkes, who have kindly allowed the portraits of Walter and Amelia Fawkes to be reproduced. Likewise, gratitude is due to Fiona Fairfax for her permission to reproduce the portrait of Charles Fairfax of Menston. The late David Gaunt kindly provided the mid eighteenth century painting of Hawksworth Hall for reproduction in this book.

Information about the Gill family of Menston Bleachworks has been supplied by Michael Gill. The author is grateful to Vera Horner for allowing access to the archives of her ancestors the Jennings and Popplewells of Menston. Further thanks are owed to Betts Gaunt, John Varker, Eddie Mercer, Geoffrey Richardson of Bradford Golf Club, and Marjorie Little and staff at High Royds Hospital, Menston.

Further valuable assistance has been received from Jack Kell, Hazel Goodwin, Oliver Pickering, Paul Wood, Christine Dean, James and Mary Lupton, Hubert Reynolds, Simon Richmond, Richard and Elizabeth Wightman, Elizabeth Woof; and Bill Pearson and colleagues of the *Wharfedale and Airedale Observer*, Otley.

The cover illustration is reproduced by kind permission of the West Yorkshire Archive Service, Bradford.

PREFACE

Early one fine summer's morning at Farnley in 1980, I awoke from a pleasant sleep and lay in bed reflecting on the discovery, three years earlier, of a small batch of eighteenth century estate maps which had come to light during the conversion of the old Farnley Estate Office into a new cheese and delicatessen shop.

That same summer morning I received a distinct impression from a 'voice' within me which clearly said: 'Do you remember those maps? Well, there are many more of those to be found from that source'.

Without hesitating for a moment, and without bothering to wash or have breakfast, I jumped out of bed, quickly threw some clothes on, and left my home in the village square to walk in the direction of Farnley Hall. Without thinking or reflecting on my actions in any way, I walked straight into a room at the Hall and immediately saw a large assortment of rolled-up papers and parchment, lying in a series of open drawers standing on the floor. A closer inspection revealed, to my amazement, that the collection comprised no less than fifty-six old estate maps, the majority of them being of the Hawksworth and Menston district. About a third of the collection comprised hand-drawn eighteenth-century items.

It was that revelation on that summer's morning which has ultimately led to this book. The maps were found to contain a great deal of unique historical information. If I had not followed my irrational impulse that day, then this book would never have materialised. I am extremely grateful to the owners of the maps, Nicholas and Susannah Horton-Fawkes, who have kindly allowed me to examine them in detail.

Having written this book, I have no wish to be regarded as the historical 'guru' of the Menston and Hawksworth district. I would rather hope that this collection of notes and narrative compiled between summer '89 and spring '90 is seen for what it really is: simply an introduction to a rich vein of local history which still remains largely untapped and which awaits further investigation.

Some aspects of Hawksworth and Menston history have been glossed over in the following pages, and there still remains considerable research to be done. In particular, the architecture and evolution of Hawksworth village deserves much closer study;

and the details of the development of modern Menston, commencing with the arrival of the railway and the planned 'new town', are themselves worthy of considerable investigation and a possible future publication – from someone other than myself.

Readers who may wish to immerse themselves in further research relating to the locality are pointed in the direction of the archives at the Yorkshire Archaeological Society at 'Claremont', Clarendon Road, Leeds, where the extensive collection of Farnley Estate Papers is to be found, and where the ever-helpful archivists can offer their expertise and patient assistance. There are smaller but no less interesting items of Hawksworth/Menston material to be seen in the collections of the West Yorkshire Archive Service at Canal Road, Bradford and Sheepscar, Leeds.

Many individuals have contributed in a greater or lesser degree towards the compilation of this book. I sincerely hope that the acknowledgement list includes all their names; but in particular I would like to thank Hazel Goodwin, Jack Kell, Oliver Pickering and Paul Wood for scrutinising the draft text; Bryan Brown for providing most of the colour photography; and Phillipa Swanton for her contribution in the form of the excellent maps and diagrams. I am also very grateful to the late David Gaunt who allowed me to browse through his fine collection of early Hawksworth papers.

Alastair Laurence
Otley 1991

Introduction

Why a history of Menston *and* Hawksworth? the reader may well ask. Menston is essentially an urban area, closely linked to a main road and a railway, and comprising mid to late nineteenth century Victorian terrace villas mixed with a scattering of more modern homes. Only a small amount of farmland survives around the edges of the township, and the close proximity of the monumental High Royds Hospital has a strong impact on the overall character of the area. Hawksworth on the other hand – far more cut off from the main lines of communication – still manages to retain its character as a 'fossilised' eighteenth century rural hamlet, surrounded by fields, open land and the golf course. It presents a radically different appearance from Menston.

The two townships are not even located in the same valley. Hawksworth faces across Airedale and its streams flow southwards until they join the river Aire. Menston is really part of Wharfedale, and its various becks and rivulets wander northwards to mingle with the Wharfe. One of these streams, Mire Beck, forms the important boundary between Menston and Hawksworth at its upper reaches and then becomes the boundary between Menston and Guiseley lower down its course. (The name 'mire' in this context probably comes from the Old English word *maere,* meaning 'boundary'. The personal surname 'Merebeck' could be found at Menston during the fourteenth century. However, the presence of the *Tranmire* ('crane marsh') suggests that the lowlying land in the vicinity of the White Cross boundary was waterlogged as well.)

In spite of their obvious differences, the two townships of Menston and Hawksworth have had a number of features in common over the years. They were once quite closely linked, and so it is convenient to deal with both places in the same historical account. An early and important link – as early as pre-Conquest date – is the fact that both places lay within the original extensive parish of Otley. Generations of residents at both Hawksworth and 'Mensington' (as it was originally known) would have regarded Otley as the main centre for their needs, whether involving weekday shopping trips to the market there, or Sunday worship at the church. The long-standing ecclesiastical links with Otley remained as late as the middle of the nineteenth century, after which time both Menston and Hawksworth detached themselves from their mother parish.

As well as being contained within the ancient parish of Otley, both townships were once part and parcel of the Archbishop of York's feudal estate, centred at Otley Manor House. This large estate had belonged to the various archbishops from at least the ninth century. Its original size can be judged from the fact that it embraced such far-flung places as Addingham, Baildon, Guiseley and Little Timble. It is difficult to know the exact extent of local involvement by the various archbishops from age to age. We do know that between the early 1200s and early 1400s, most of the archbishops spent no more than one or two days per year at Otley Manor House, suggesting that they had little or no personal interest in their Otley-based lands other than as a source of income.

By the thirteenth century, various parts of the manor had been granted out to the so-called 'mesne' lords – that is, those 'intermediate' landlords who, whilst recognising the archbishop of the day as being nominally their 'overlord' and holding their lands from him by service, nevertheless had tenants of their own and had a strong say in local affairs. Included among the early Wharfedale mesne lords were the Mansell family, who held Burley with part of 'Mensington' in the twelfth and thirteenth centuries; and the Lindley family, who held the vill of Lindley and half of Farnley during the early fourteenth century. At the same period, the Hawksworth portion of the archbishop's estate formed part of the holdings of the Warde family, who were also influential at nearby Guiseley and Esholt. A marriage between Beatrice Warde and a certain Walter de Hawksworth, sometime in the mid 1200s, helped to establish the Hawksworths as eventual successors to the Wardes by the year 1315.

As the centuries passed by, so the local influence and power of the various archbishops gradually waned. By the end of the seventeenth century, the steward at Otley was able to obtain only the paltry rental of 1s 11d from certain lands at Menston still regarded as being within 'Bishop's Bounds'. A deed of 1655 names a field at Menston as Bishop Lands. A group of fields called Bishop Briggs still exist on the boundary between Hawksworth and Menston. There is preserved in the Gaunt Papers a written receipt from the steward at Otley, dated the 29th September 1664, in which he states to have 'Recd then of Walter Hawksworth Esq the sum of 6/- due to his Grace the Lord Archbishop of Yorke at ye feast of St Michaell ye Archangell for halfe years rent due for several closes called Stubbing in Hawksworth within ye Manor of Otley'. This receipt shows that the archbishop still retained some degree of overlordship at this relatively late date.

A further strong historical link between Menston and Hawksworth can be found in the names of the families who populated the locality in previous centuries. The most commonly found of these surnames appears to be that of Rhodes, who, having originated themselves at High Rhodes by the thirteenth century, spread out and established branches at all adjacent townships; and so we find numerous Rhodes at both Menston and Hawksworth throughout the sixteenth, seventeenth, eighteenth and nineteenth centuries. Other local families whose names appear in both townships include the Hawksworths, Jennings, Marshalls, Mittons, Pickards, Popplewells, Rileys, Wards and Watsons. This book contains accounts of other long-established families, such as the Nichols of Norcroft, the Hitches of Menston Grange, and the Breary, Exley, Fairfax and Fourness families who lived along Main Street, Menston.

Perhaps the strongest connection between Hawksworth and Menston is the fact that the Hawksworth family of Hawksworth Hall held lands in Menston village from the thirteenth century onwards. Their earliest possessions appeared to be Hagwood Farm on the borders of Burley, and half of High Rhodes. These farms had been acquired around 1260 by Walter de Hawksworth from Ralph Mansell of Burley and Robert Faukes of Wakefield (whose brother, William Faukes of Newall, Otley, was the ancestor of the Farnley Fawkes). The Hawksworths extended their influence at Menston during the early seventeenth century by purchasing lands there from the Greene family. In 1629, Sir Richard Hawksworth's tenants in Menston village were named as Ralph Curtis (the principal tenant, paying £5 rent per annum), Richard Ward of the Tofts, Thomas Thompson also of the Tofts, and Thomas Rhodes of Waitlands.

It was not until the mid-eighteenth century that the Hawksworths made major inroads into Menston. In 1753 they purchased Low Hall and its lands from the executors of John Rhodes; in 1763 they acquired Menston Old Hall and 112 acres of former Fairfax farmland; and in 1773 the large expanse of open, rough grazing land known as Menston Common was enclosed, the majority of the newly-enclosed fields being allocated to Walter Hawksworth. (The original extent of the old common and the various land holdings in the eighteenth century can be seen in the map which appears later in this book.) By the end of the eighteenth century, the only parts of Menston which lay outside the Hawksworths' domain were the Grange, half of High Rhodes and two or three smallholdings in the main street, such as Moor Croft and Fourness House.

Shortly after 1786 the Hawksworths left their ancestral home. In accordance with the wishes of their kinsman, Francis Fawkes of Farnley (who was the last of the original Fawkes), the Hawksworths moved to Farnley Hall and added the surname of Fawkes to their own. In so doing, they were entitled, under the terms of the will of Francis Fawkes, to inherit his lands at Farnley, Newall, Lindley, Norwood, Stainburn, Castley, Pool and Otley. For the next eighty-six years both Hawksworth town and Menston town formed an integral part of this extensive Farnley Estate; and all the old Hawksworth family documents and muniments (including those maps stumbled across by the writer of this account) were moved to Farnley, the new administrative centre of the Estate. Around the time of this removal, various artefacts of sentimental value were understandably extracted from Hawksworth Hall. These included armorial painted glass and a large panelled fireplace surround. From Menston Old Hall some years later (1814) were removed a formal stone gateway and wall, a stone corner fireplace bearing the initials of Charles Fairfax and the date 1657, and the so-called Cromwell garden table. These too were taken to Farnley.

In 1871, Ayscough Hawksworth Fawkes (1831–99) inherited the Farnley Estate. The following year his solicitors Constable and Maskell of Otley noted that 'Mr Fawkes is desirous of selling his estate in Menston with a view to freeing the rest of his estates from a great portion of the family charges'. The sale of the Menston lands had obviously become necessary to satisfy various family legacies and debts. 1872 was a good year to contemplate a sale – the railway had recently arrived, the construction of a new station at Menston was in hand, and the area was ripe for development. Auction plans were drawn up, and a new street system was mapped out in the fields of Menston village. Modern Menston was born.

Who was responsible for the concept and layout of the new Menston, we do not know. The building plots were organised within and around a framework of new streets named Park Road, Station Road, Farnley Road and Cleasby Road, the latter name possibly being chosen by Ayscough Fawkes' wife Edith Mary, who was the daughter of Sir Anthony Cleasby. The auctions took place between June 1873 and September 1876, and by the latter date little remained of the Fawkes' Menston property, apart from Old Hall farm, tenanted by the Popplewells, which was eventually sold some nineteen years later.

Meanwhile, over the hill at Hawksworth, nothing changed. The essentially early eighteenth century character of the village was preserved intact by virtue of the fact that little or no rebuilding or modernisation was carried out. It was from 1872, then, that the two townships began to diverge in character, Menston becoming a modern railway suburb, Hawksworth remaining an undeveloped rural backwater. However, both places still retained one or two features in common, and an important one of these was the presence of flourishing Methodism.

Local Methodist records show that both Hawksworth and Menston were active in the very early days of the Society, Menston leading the way by commencing weekly meetings in 1744, with Hawksworth following about sixteen years later. The reason behind Menston's early start may have been the fact that Jonathan Maskew, the earliest recorded local Methodist minister, hailed from nearby Stead at Burley Woodhead. Maskew began his ministry around 1743. He was sent by the Reverend William Grimshaw of Haworth to preach and evangelize in the townships around his native village. On reaching Guiseley, Maskew drew the attention of a gang of local louts, who violently assaulted him, tore the clothes off his back, and dragged him along the gravelled roadway. Rescue came in the shape of a handful of local residents who luckily were more accommodating than their neighbours; and Jonathan Maskew is believed to have settled at Menston for some time, founding the first group of Methodists there.

At Menston, Maskew would have come into contact with a certain Isaac Brown of neighbouring Hawksworth; and Brown emulated Maskew by entering the ministry in 1760. He became an early superintendent of the great Haworth Round of itinerant preachers, and spent forty-three years travelling for the Methodist cause. Brown was well known to John Wesley, the founder of Methodism, who spoke of him as 'honest Isaac Brown' and who thought highly of his evangelistic ability. In 1803 Brown retired to Pontefract, apparently until his death in 1814. However, a survey for Hawksworth dated 1811 shows a house in the village (which still stands today) to be occupied by one Isaac Brown. Did he return to his native village in his old age?

The first Methodist chapel was erected at Menston in 1826, largely as a result of the efforts of Robert Exley, a member of a yeoman cloth-making family who had lived at High Rhodes.

Exley's father, Thomas, had purchased a farm known as Moor Croft in 1797, and it was in a corner of this farm that the chapel was built, with a burial ground added five years later. At Hawksworth, the first chapel, dating from 1832, replaced earlier meetings held at local homes, such as that of George Raistrick, licensed for preaching in 1786.

Leading nineteenth century nonconformist families included the Rennards, Naylors, Popplewells and Raistricks at Hawksworth, and the Exley, Jennings, Hodgson, Clough, Watmough, Muschamp and Hanson families from Menston. By the middle of the century, most of the farming tenantry were big Methodists. This fact helps to explain why a long-established village alehouse at Hawksworth – the Brown Cow – had its doors permanently shut later in the century as a result of a village petition! It may also explain why the farmers' landlords, the Farnley Fawkes, were reluctant to become patrons of the new Anglican St John's church at Menston (1870–1).

Until its 'new town' building boom of the 1870s, Menston always had a smaller number of residents than Hawksworth. For example, in 1822 the population of Menston was 257; that of Hawksworth, 323. In spite of this, early industrial enterprises flourished at Menston far more than at Hawksworth, which remained based on a purely agricultural footing. Of particular importance at Menston for many years was the domestic wool-combing trade. The township was unusual when compared with many surrounding places because of its link-up with the Bradford-based worsted industry, whereas other local textile towns such as Guiseley, Yeadon and Rawdon were essentially based on the domestic weaving of woollen cloth.

By the middle of the nineteenth century, over 110 Menston residents worked at home, producing worsted fibres and preparing them for eventual machine spinning at either Greenholme Mills, Burley, or Ackroyd's Mill, Otley. The process of wool-combing was then a very labour-intensive operation, and this helps to explain why so many Menston residents were kept hard at it. The hand-operated combs, used to separate the long worsted fibres (the tops) from the discarded shorter ones (the noils) had to be treated in cinder fires, and the familiar trademark of a Menston comber's cottage was the possession of a black sooty ceiling. Woolcombing was done at all parts of the village – at farms, or in the rows of cottages around Derry Hill, some of which are now demolished. At Hill Top Farm, a specially-built combing shop had been con-

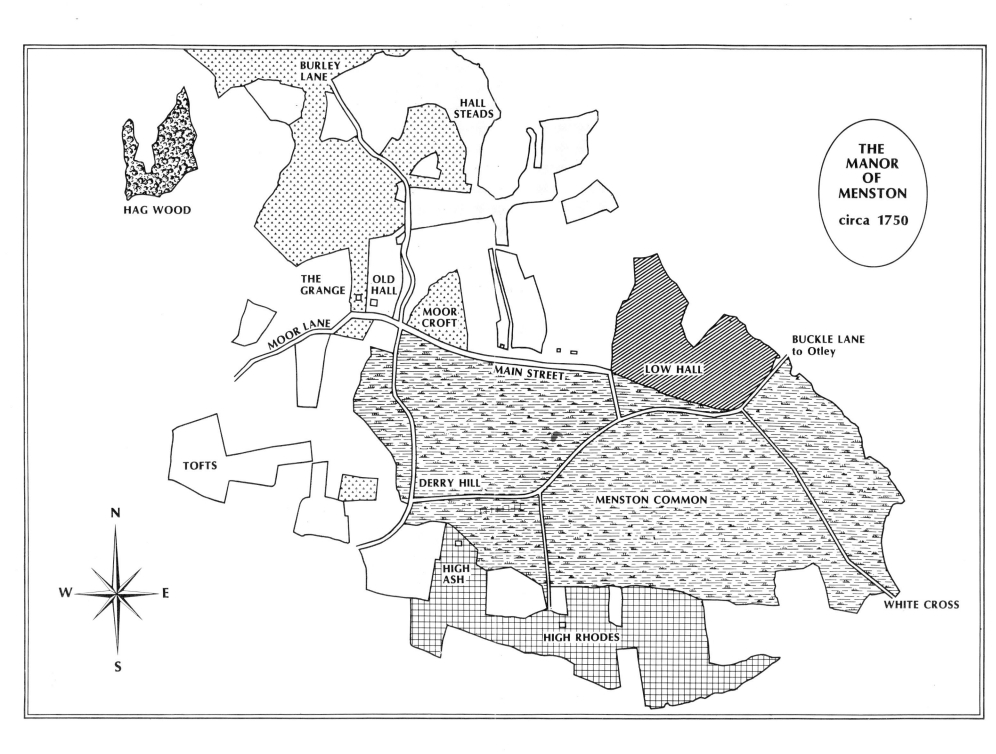

THE
MANOR
OF
MENSTON

circa 1750

HAG WOOD

BURLEY
LANE

HALL
STEADS

THE
GRANGE

OLD
HALL

MOOR
CROFT

MOOR LANE

MAIN STREET

LOW HALL

BUCKLE LANE
to Otley

TOFTS

DERRY HILL

MENSTON COMMON

HIGH
ASH

HIGH RHODES

WHITE CROSS

N
W   E
S

THE MANOR OF MENSTON circa 1750

 Low Hall, Rhodes family, seventeenth and eighteenth centuries. Sold by the executors of John Rhodes to Walter Hawksworth in 1753.

 Fairfax lands, seventeenth and eighteenth centuries, based on the Old Hall. Sold by David Middleton and Elizabeth his wife (née Fairfax) to the trustees of Walter Hawksworth, 1763.

 Menston Common, a large expanse of rough grazing land, not enclosed until 1773. The newly partitioned lands then allocated to Walter Hawksworth etc.

 Menston Grange and Moor Croft, More and Hitch families, etc.

 High Rhodes and High Ash Farms, Rhodes family and their descendants from time immemorial until 1815.

 Woodland cover in 1750.

structed next to the farmhouse and barn by William Marshall in 1851.

Suddenly, all the small hives of domestic industry at Menston ceased, for in 1857 Ackroyds of Otley built a gigantic wool-combing shed (today occupied by Smith Settle, the publishers of this book) and installed the newly-invented woolcombing machines. The laborious cottage processes at Menston quickly slipped into oblivion, and the out-of-work combers had to find employment at the local mills. After 1860, we see a healthy diversification of textile occupations among Menston house-holders, and by 1871 the community included worsted weavers (15), mule spinners (14), overlookers (11), woollen cloth weavers (9), carder fillers (5), cloth millers (2), a wool sorter and a tweed weaver. It was also during the 1860s that a new breed made its appearance: the bleacher. A dozen or so local residents now found employment at the Rombaldsmoor Bleachworks of Joseph Gill and Sons. During the 1860s and 70s, new sources of employment were found – on the railway and in the quarrying and masonry work associated with the construction and development of Menston new town.

Like every English village, Hawksworth possessed a cluster of trades essential for the running of the rural economy. Joiners, wheelwrights, blacksmiths and stonemasons would always find plentiful ongoing work among the farmers. At Hawksworth, we do find a few unusual trades, however. The Mitton family were specialists in the home-weaving of linen fabric during the eight-eenth century. Their neighbours the Popplewells made shovels. (There survives in the Gaunt Papers a lease of Tranmire Farm from Walter Hawksworth to William Popplewell of Guiseley, shovel maker, dated the 21st February 1753. William's contemporary, Stephen Popplewell, was already established at Hawksworth as a blacksmith.)

During the 1730s the Boococks and Reynards of Hawksworth had a go at 'dish throwing', but their small enterprise never really took off. Richard Barrett was busy in the village as a 'fishmonger' in the middle of the eighteenth century. We are not sure where he obtained his fish from, nor how he kept his produce fresh – perhaps he was a salter and dryer of fish caught in the pre-industrial river Aire and a forerunner of the modern Harry Ramsden.

Moving forward in time to the 1880s, a major development took place at Menston which was awe-inspiring in its magnitude, yet at the same time ominous and even frightening for many local residents. The third County 'Pauper Lunatic Asylum' – as it was then known – was constructed on a 287 acre site, much of which had once been part of the old Menston Common. Francis Rhodes Darwin of Creskeld Hall, Arthington, was the person chiefly responsible for the choice of the hospital site. Darwin's distant ancestors were in fact the Rhodes of High Rhodes.

Harry Speight, writing in 1900, commented that Menston now had 'melancholy fame as the scene of the latest County Lunatic Asylum, yet it is a pleasure to reflect that in this huge institution, whose magnificent gables and towers are a conspicuous landmark for many miles round, every provision is made for the comfort and well-being of the patients'. Those 'magnificent gables', part of the ambitious design of Mr Edwards, the county surveyor, were certainly produced by great toil and hardship, for the workmen resident on the hospital building site, who were forced to stop work for three months because of the severe winter weather of 1886, reached near-starvation point. A locally-funded soup kitchen saved them. For more details of the construction of the hospital, the reader is referred to the contemporary reports from the *Wharfedale and Airedale Observer*, which appear in Appendix 6.

The last, and by no means least, feature which Menston and Hawksworth have in common is that they exist in surroundings of pleasant, interesting, and in places spectacular landscape and scenery. The magnificent Todhaw is perhaps best viewed from upper Yeadon, from where it appears like the belly of a gigantic whale, and where it can be compared with its 'sister', Yeadon Haw. The wild, lonely and remote valley through which runs Mire Beck in the territory between Hawksworth and Menston offers surprising solitude in a locality close to well-populated zones of housing. Headley Bank near Southpiece, Menston, is an imposing but little-known cliff, on the top of which is a large plateau, the kind of plateau which suggests itself as the site of very early human settlement. Craven Hall Hill on Hawksworth Moor looks gaunt and foreboding to the person who approaches it in order to toil up to its summit; but from its heights a most wonderful vista unfolds, one which should be experienced by each and every Menstonian and Hawksworthian at least once in their lifetime. On the borders of Esholt and Hawksworth, the curious Hawkstone, from which the village of Hawksworth is believed to take its name, stands almost forgotten in a small wood. For many of the residents of nearby Tranmere Park, who may be familiar with the more exotic parts of France, Spain, Italy or Greece, the Hawkstone on their doorsteps is surprisingly unknown.

As this book was in the process of being compiled, a large amount of information came to light. A number of new historical riddles reared their heads, and a few old unanswered questions still remain unanswered. For instance, the boundary marker known as White Cross was once a well-known landmark, where the three townships of Guiseley, Hawksworth and Menston met. Was the original White Cross in fact a limestone 'erratic', a standing boulder of whitish stone which had been dragged down-valley during the last Ice Age by the action of the same glacier which created the trough called Guiseley Gap?

Running across Hawksworth Moor is the long, straight boundary line between Hawksworth and Burley Woodhead. From as early as the thirteenth century, this line was locally known as York Way. Are we in fact looking here at the alignment of a long-lost Roman military road, or even an ancient overland trade route? The name York Way is long forgotten, as is another road name, Craven Street, occurring at Menston in the early fourteenth century. It is quite possible that York Way and Craven Street were synonymous, being parts of the same routeway crossing through the township. The name Craven Hall Hill can be found on the modern Ordnance Survey map of Hawksworth Moor. It may be of significance that this place name occurs close to the position of York Way.

Does the preponderance of distinctly Danish field names at Menston also have any significance? The Tofts, Briskers (probably *birk scough* – 'birch wood'), Carl Rein, Rainey Croft and nearby Thorpe are all names of probable Danish origin. The flat table-lands that characterize the immediate Menston locality may have been selected by Danish settlers as being particularly suitable for swine rearing and feeding. Until the late eighteenth century, a large proportion of Menston remained as one large, flattish, undrained area of uncultivated wasteland. This particular landscape feature might have appealed to a Danish pig farmer, whereas an Anglo-Saxon tiller might have preferred arable lands in the valley bottoms, and the Norse shepherds might choose to site their settlement on the edge of moorland sheep pastures.

Was the obscure medieval settlement called Chapel Croft on the boundary of Hawksworth and Menston, recorded as early as 1273, the location of an ecclesiastical building? Or is it more likely that this name was given because the rent from the lands here provided an endowment for a chantry chapel in either Otley or Guiseley church? There was a medieval chapel at Hawksworth Hall, but its exact location is now uncertain. The 'chapel chamber' was still there in 1657. At Menston, there appears to be some local importance attached to Saint John. For example, the Rhodes Charity, founded in 1751, was distributed annually among local residents on St John's Day; and the first-known Anglican place of worship in the village, the cottage in Derry Hill, was licensed in 1858 and named as the Chapel of St John the Divine. This name was later transferred to the new church (1870–1).

One of the oft-repeated tales which emerges from time to time at Menston is the one about the elusive secret tunnel from the seventeenth-century Menston Grange to the seventeenth-century Old Hall. It is hard to believe that such a tunnel exists. The Hitch family of the Grange were Royalists, and their neighbours the Fairfaxes at the Old Hall were leading Parliamentarians – so there would have been no particular need for any link-up. If clandestine visits or 'escapes' were necessary, then the blackness of seventeenth century night time was almost as effective as a tunnel; and what Menston resident would wish to spend hundreds of valuable hours underground hacking their way through 400 yards of clay? The Grange has a very fine, well-built cellar complete with a shallow well in its flagged floor. Perhaps the existence of this well led to fantasies about tunnels?

On a similar theme, are the mysterious 'priest holes' at Hawksworth Hall really what they are claimed to be? Or is it more likely that the small hollows, gaps and cavities found behind panelling there are the results of simple domestic remodelling, such as the replacement of a large open hearth and fire-screen with a smaller chimney and panelled fireplace? Although William Hawksworth (died 1588) was apparently imprisoned for his Catholic recusancy, the Hawksworths who were living in the seventeenth century when the present hall was built were not only Anglican – they were Puritan as well; and so a 'priest hole' of some kind or other is hardly likely to have been called for.

The Hawkstone

A rocky outcrop of gritstone overlooks the main road from White Cross to Shipley. Most of the rock formation cannot be seen from the road itself – it hides behind a belt of private woodland plantation – but from the summit of the principal boulder, the giant Hawkstone, a spectacular vista of Airedale opens up. Although the Hawkstone is actually within the township of Esholt and a few hundred yards away from the old boundary line with Hawksworth, there is reason to believe that the place name

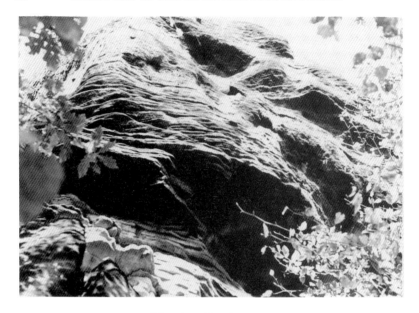

The giant Hawkstone.

element 'hawk' in 'Hawksworth' owes its original derivation to this stone.

The south-east face of the chief boulder is seen by some as reminiscent of the head of a hawk. A dimple high up on the rock suggests a cold, brooding 'eye', and small cracks and fissures conjure up the lines of a 'beak'. Towards the base of the rock face is a flat shelf of stone which leads into an intriguing naturally-formed weather-worn roofed shelter, directly under the 'head' of the hawk. There appears to be only one local folk tale attached to the stone: it tells of how a hunter on horseback, perhaps losing his way, galloped his horse clean over the edge and plunged to his death many feet below in the bracken.

The Golf Course

Bradford Golf Club, which occupies the Hawksworth links, has its origins at Baildon in 1891. At that date, the club was known as 'Bradford St Andrew's Golf Club', and its membership was unusual in that it was then exclusively for Scotsmen who had become domiciled in the Bradford area.

In 1898 the club, now open to players from south of the border, moved to Hawksworth to occupy the seventy acre parkland known as Hall Croft immediately to the south of the hall. The golfers entered into a twenty year lease in January 1899 with the landlords, the Fawkes of Farnley, paying an annual rent of £184 16s. At the same time a newly-built clubhouse was formally opened by the politician A J Balfour MP, who was to become Prime Minister two years later. (The original building was destroyed by fire in 1925, and following extensive rebuilding work, a new clubhouse was opened in 1926.)

When the Hawksworth Estate was broken up into lots for sale by auction in 1919, the golf club was able to purchase the grounds privately for the sum of £5,000. Some years later the size of the golf course was extended by the acquisition of a further forty or so acres towards the east.

Thorpe

Thorpe now consists of a single farmhouse and an adjoining barn perched on a prominent mound, off Thorpe Lane, overlooking the Guiseley Gap and surrounded by two or three large grassy fields; but the landscape at Thorpe has changed dramatically over the past 200 years: the thirty or so small enclosures, crofts and paddocks which once surrounded a cluster of houses here have long vanished, with most of the houses, to be transformed into large areas of somewhat featureless grassland.

Thorpe has been identified as the location of the former settlement called 'Little Hawksworth' which was named as one of the berewicks or outlying villages attached to the Archbishop of York's Otley manor in 1030. The distinctly Danish name 'Thorpe' (meaning an outlying satellite settlement attached to a larger one) exactly describes the relationship of Little Hawksworth to its mother settlement of Over Hawksworth, higher up the hill. The comparative sizes of the two Hawksworths can be estimated from the fact that Sir Richard Hawksworth could in 1629 extract a rental of £65 6s 4d from his tenants at Over Hawksworth, whereas his farms at 'Thorpe alias little Hawksworth' yielded £21 6s 3d.

Among the residents of Thorpe (1629) were members of the Rhodes, Whittingham, Pollard, Nelson, Cowling, Maude, Thompson, Binns and Bolton families. This list of names is suggestive of a thriving and well-populated hamlet. By the early nineteenth century, Thorpe had been reduced to two farmholdings – the low one held by the Kettlewells and Popplewells, and the higher one (based on the present farmhouse) being occupied by the Todd, Rhodes and Popplewell families.

In 1919, Thorpe farm, along with the two neighbouring farms of Norcroft and Odda, was sold by Frederick Hawksworth Fawkes to the West Riding County Council for incorporation into the Menston Hospital Estate. In recent years the farm has become the property of the Ogden Group of Companies.

The Early Hawksworths

The history of the family who took their name from Hawksworth has been well documented. Herald's Visitation pedigrees survive from the seventeenth century; and a very detailed family tree was printed in Whitaker's *History of Leeds,* published in the early nineteenth century. Whitaker's information begins with the statement that the first person bearing the surname Hawksworth came over with William the Conqueror and was killed at the Battle of Hastings. This assertion is likely to have been a fabrication by one of the seventeenth century heralds. The truth about the origin of the family is less romantic and more down-to-earth, but no less interesting to the local historian: the Hawksworths were part of a race of Scandinavians who settled, probably peacefully rather than with any conquering force, in a corner of the Archbishop of York's Otley estate a century or so before the Norman Conquest.

In the twelfth century we find three individuals living at Hawksworth bearing the simple, rustic and very un-English names of Gamel, Toki and Thurstan. This odd group must have existed as farmers of upland pastures which were relatively remote and isolated from the main centres. The late survival of such distinctive Scandinavian personal names (which also occur at Stainburn, in similar hill country) does suggest that the inhabitants of Hawksworth were cut off, culturally speaking, from their neighbours for a long period of time, and in so being they preserved some kind of Scandinavian continuity.

Of the three named individuals, Toki had a son called Lenard de Hawksworth, who is mentioned in a deed of circa 1200; and Thurstan had two sons, Hugh and William de Hawksworth, living around the same time. In the year 1248 another member of the same family, Siward de Hawksworth, appears on the scene, bearing yet another Scandinavian name. A Robert de Hawksworth, living in 1227, had a son described in contemporary deeds as 'Thomas le Russ de Haukeswrd'. This Thomas was a founder of a branch of the family who eventually bore the surname Rouse. It is likely that Thomas and other members of his family were given the additional surname because of their distinctive red hair – another possible pointer to Viking origin of the family. In 1281, a certain Robert Rufus dwelt at High Rhodes, Menston; and by 1322 Hugh 'le Rous', son of Robert, was living at or near 'Todhaw' (Todda) immediately above the village of Hawksworth.

The first-known Walter de Hawksworth makes his appearance in a deed of about 1220. He was one of the sons of Robert de Hawksworth and therefore a brother of Thomas le Russ. From this date onwards, the Christian name Walter was to be chosen by many successive generations of the family. This fact makes it very difficult, if not impossible, to construct a totally exact early family pedigree, as it is all too easy, when reading the early muniments, to confuse one Walter with another Walter belonging to a different generation. There is one particular early Walter, however, who does stick out in the records: he was the one who married Beatrice Warde sometime in the mid-thirteenth century, and in so doing brought the manor and lordship of Hawksworth into the hands of his own family by the year 1273.

The link-up between the Wardes and the Hawksworths needs explaining further. Throughout the twelfth and thirteenth centuries, the Wardes were without doubt the leading family at Guiseley, Esholt and Hawksworth. Originally from Givendale, near Ripon, the Wardes eventually made their home base locally, probably at the moated Esholt Old Hall. Simon Warde of Givendale, living in the mid-twelfth century, gave lands in Esholt to Sinningthwaite Priory, a grant which was confirmed by Simon's son William later in the century. Undoubtedly the priory of St Leonards was built upon part of this Esholt land, adjacent to the river Aire. William was succeeded by Sir Simon Warde, who married Constance de Vescy around 1210. Of their seven children – William, Nicholas, Simon, Alice, Isabel, Beatrice and Joan – the youngest son, Simon, became a rector of Guiseley church; and Beatrice married Walter de Hawksworth.

It is quite likely that the Wardes were responsible for establishing the parish church at Guiseley. If this was not so, then at least they were its principal benefactors and patrons for six or more generations. Simon Warde, Rector of Guiseley, was succeeded by his nephew Nicholas, also named as Rector of Guiseley in 1282. Nicholas in turn was succeeded by his nephew, another Nicholas Warde, rector in 1307. (Lengthy biographical details about the Warde family appeared in Philemon Slater's *History of the Ancient Parish of Guiseley*. The information, supplied by one Horatio

Ward of London, is unfortunately a confusing mish-mash of inaccuracy.)

There survives in the Gaunt Papers a seventeenth century copy of a deed dated 1273 between Simon, son of Simon Warde, and his relative Walter, son of Walter of Hawksworth (which is reproduced in translation from the original Latin as part of Appendix 3 in this book). This important charter confirms that Simon had given and granted to his kinsman Walter 'all my land and rents in the vill of Hawksworth'. We can guess that the marriage of Walter to Beatrice Warde had enabled this gift to take place. The deed is particularly interesting as it describes the boundaries of the township and recites a series of fascinating place-names. It has been possible to track down all of these place-names – they are shown in the map opposite.

The *Nomina Villarum* of 1315–16 names Walter de Hawksworth as Lord of the Manor of Hawksworth, a proud title his descendants were to retain until 1919. The Hawksworths eventually took over the role of the Wardes as far as the rectory of Guiseley was concerned – John de Hawksworth being appointed rector there on the 16th September 1349 and remaining until 1371; but the patronage of Guiseley church stayed in the hands of the Wardes for a further 170 years until the death of Sir Christopher Warde in 1522. It was rector John de Hawksworth who used the earliest-known representation of the family coat of arms – in the form of a wax seal portraying three hawks. Whether he was actually the first to use this emblem, we do not know.

Six years prior to John de Hawksworth's appointment at Guiseley, the Hawksworths had obtained a licence from the Archbishop of York for their chapel at Hawksworth, probably a new edifice within or near to the Hall. The close chronological coincidence of the chapel with John's rectorship does suggest that the family were of particularly ecclesiastical orientation at this date. For further details about the medieval chapel in question, see the following section on Hawksworth Hall and also Appendix 1.

In the early fourteenth century, one of the Walter de Hawksworths married Isabella Sotherton, the daughter of Sir John Sotherton; and as a result of this alliance the Hawksworths acquired the manor and estate of Mitton, a village on the River Ribble at the old border of Yorkshire and Lancashire. The Hawksworths may have moved to Mitton (which had belonged to the Sothertons), because evidence of their existence at Hawksworth is very sparse during the second half of the fourteenth century and early fifteenth. The poll tax return of 1379 shows no

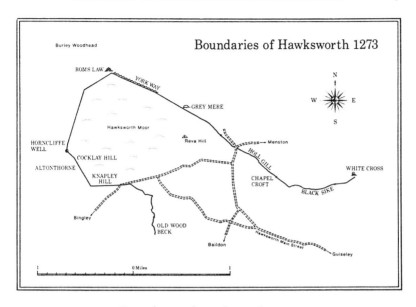

Boundaries of Hawksworth 1273

member of the Hawksworth family actually living at Hawksworth. This may be explained by the fact that the family were domiciled at Mitton.

By the early fifteenth century the family also owned a house in the city of York, and so their time spent in the country at Hawksworth may have been spasmodic if not at all. Further evidence of to-ing and fro-ing between Mitton and Hawksworth is suggested by the existence of a family surnamed Mitton who lived at Hawksworth from at least the early sixteenth century until the early nineteenth. This long-established yeoman family, specialists in the hand-weaving of linen by the eighteenth century, must have originated from Mitton and came over to Hawksworth as a result of the Sotherton connection.

In 1440, the Hawksworth of the day, one Thomas, was living at York. He leased 'the site and mansion of his manor at Hawksworth with all his demesne lands to the said manor belonging' to his son and heir, John. This lease contains the earliest-known reference to a building subsequently known as Hawksworth Hall, a predecessor of the present building and doubtless on or very near the same site. There survives the will of a Thomas Hawksworth of

York, dated the 17th May 1447; and we believe this individual to be the one and the same Thomas who leased Hawksworth Hall to his son seven years earlier. In his will, Thomas requested to be buried at York, in the church of the Friars Preachers. This evidence suggests that the Hawksworths were well-settled at York. When John the son himself died in 1464, the administration of his goods and chattels was granted to a certain Edmund Lound of Mitton, once again suggesting well-established personal links with, and probable residence at, Mitton.

For further information about the early Hawksworths, the reader is referred to the very detailed account which is to be found in W Paley Baildon's two volume book, *Baildon and the Baildons*. Although this impressive book was published over fifty years ago and is hard to come by, a few copies may still be found in local reference libraries.

The Later Hawksworths

The history of the later Hawksworths could be said to begin with the building of the earliest part of the present Hawksworth Hall during the time of Walter and Isabel Hawksworth in the early seventeenth century. By that date, the family had been associated with the village for over 400 years, a period during which the Christian name Walter had become so well-established that it would be something of an understatement to say that it was a popular name with the family. No fewer than nine direct ancestors of the early seventeenth century Walter were also Walters. (Curiously enough, there is now living a Mr Walter Hawksworth of Heaton Drive, Baildon, in whose family there is a general understanding that their ancestors were from Hawksworth!)

As the family was once quite numerous locally, not all of its members would live at the hall. A leading branch dwelt at Menston during the fourteenth and fifteenth centuries, where they inter-married with the Brearys; another branch lived at Tranmires, the old stone house still standing in Thorpe Lane, until the late seventeenth century; and yet another branch, that founded by William Hawksworth (died 1603), was at Hope Farm, Baildon. This William was a younger brother of the Walter for whom Hawksworth Hall was rebuilt in the early seventeenth century.

Another younger brother of this same generation (viz Walter and William's) was Peter Hawksworth, the seventh son. He moved to Thornbury, Gloucestershire, where he died in the 1640s. His descendants emigrated to Ireland around the year 1690 and stayed there until 1834. Returning to England, the family settled in Dorset. Some 350 years after their original departure from Yorkshire, they returned to their ancestral county, in the form of the late Peter Hawkesworth and his family of Aldbrough, where they settled in 1962. Peter's son, Simon Hawkesworth of Knaresborough, has provided useful and interesting family information which has been used in this book. The Gloucester/Ireland/Dorset branch of the family retain an earlier spelling of the surname (with the additional 'e').

Returning to the Hawksworths at the hall, Isabel was able to enjoy her new house for only a short spell, for she died in 1612, a year after the building was completed. Her husband Walter died in 1620, to be buried in Otley Church. The couple were succeeded by their eldest son Richard, a great individualist, a strong character, but one who also possessed a temperament which was reputedly quarrelsome, aggressive and even cruel.

Richard received a knighthood in his late twenties. This honour does not seem to have been awarded for any particular public service: rather, it was probably of a compulsory nature and would have been gained by a monetary payment to the Crown. Sir Richard was married twice. His first wife, Anne Wentworth of Elmsall, died soon after giving birth to their only child, Katherine. Richard married secondly Mary Goodricke, the daughter of Sir Henry Goodricke of Ribston; and it is in the events leading to the breakdown of this second marriage that some aspects of Sir Richard's personality reveal themselves.

The trouble flared up in 1627, when Mary Hawksworth was forced to flee the matrimonial home, taking with her the two young children Jane and Walter. According to the allegations of the Goodricke family, the reason for her departure from Hawksworth was the result of cruelty on the part of her husband. The Goodrickes petitioned the Archbishop of York, a personal friend, to intervene in the matter – possibly to attempt a reconciliation but also to use his influence to enable the Goodrickes to have custody of the children. In support of their case, the Goodrickes claimed, in 1631, that Sir Richard had failed to provide his wife with alimony since the separation; they suggested that 'Sir Richard had but servants in his house of vulgar condition and the boy being four years of age was like to take impressions of his surroundings to his great harm'; and they further went on to point out that 'the child of Sir Richard's former wife was not trusted to him but was handed over to the grandfather'. This child would have been Katherine Hawksworth, a daughter by Anne Wentworth.

In his defence, Sir Richard claimed that his wife, under the strong influence of her mother, was made 'more forward' so that 'in short time she grew so respectless and insolent towards him, and her carriage and demeanour therein not so provident for this defendant's good as she might and ought to have been, that he refused to let her control the estate, and would no longer suffer her as before to dispose of it. Whereat she conceived such displeasure that she departed from this defendant's said dwelling place at Hawksworth'.

It appears that the couple were never reconciled, and the archbishop granted the Goodrickes a licence giving them custody of the two young children. By 1632, Sir Richard had spent £500 on lawsuits over the differences with his wife. Between 1632 and his death, he was involved in at least fifteen separate cases in the law courts, an indication of the extent of his quarrelsome personality. It has been claimed that the children never set foot in Hawksworth Hall until after their father's death in 1657; but this assertion is contradicted by Sir Richard's inventory, made shortly after his death, which shows that the Hall contained a 'Young Mr Chamber', meaning a bedroom used by Sir Richard's son Walter, and a 'Mr Bayldon Chamber', another similar room used by Sir Richard's daughter Jane and her husband Francis Baildon of Baildon. If there was no reconciliation with his wife, then at least Sir Richard appeared to have been in close contact with his children at a later period.

At the outbreak of the Civil War in 1642, Sir Richard Hawksworth declared himself for Parliament. In doing so, he allied himself with the Fairfaxes of neighbouring Menston and one or two of the local Puritan gentry such as the Dyneleys of Bramhope and the Stanhopes of Horsforth. The majority of the remaining gentry families of the locality, particularly the more conservative and Roman Catholic orientated, were loyal to King Charles. These included the Vavasours of Weston, the Fawkes of Farnley and the Palmes of Lindley. However, Sir Richard was prevented from playing an active part in the early days of the Civil War, for at the time of the first Siege of Bradford in December 1642 a Royalist detachment of horse arrived at Hawksworth and immediately arrested him. The person who had instigated this action was Sir John Goodricke, commander of a troop of Royalist horse, who was in fact Sir Richard's brother-in-law. It looks as though this act may have been one of deliberate revenge for the earlier treatment of Goodricke's sister Mary at Hawksworth. Sir Richard was thrown into prison at York, where he remained captive for some twenty months until the city surrendered to the Parliamentary forces after the battle of Marston Moor in July 1644.

Sir Richard died 'of ye palsy' at Hawksworth on the 11th February 1657 and was buried at Otley. His successor at the hall was his only son, Walter, then aged about thirty-two, and Walter's wife Alice Brownlowe. Walter appeared to share the same Puritan leanings as his father, for he was named in 1649 as one of the founding trustees of the well-known Puritan chapel at Bramhope, established by the Dyneleys. We know little else about this Walter and his wife Alice, apart from one important detail: we know that they were responsible for greatly enlarging the size of Hawksworth Hall during the 1660s – the eastern half of the house and the barn to the rear appear to have been erected during their time. (For further details about this, see the next section on Hawksworth Hall.) Alice died in 1675 and her husband Walter followed two years later at the early age of fifty-two.

The hall was left in the hands of a young lad, seventeen year old Walter Hawksworth, the only surviving child of Walter and Alice, whose brief life (he unfortunately died at the very young age of twenty-two) was certainly mercurial and somewhat extraordinary. At the age of eighteen he met and married Anne Markham, the seventh daughter of Sir Robert Markham of Sedgebrook, Lincoln-shire. According to a contemporary account, the couple had met, married and had the marriage consummated all within twenty-four hours! While still a teenager, Walter was created a baronet by Charles II. Like the knighthood granted to Walter's grandfather, Richard, this titular honour (which was a hereditary one) was awarded to eligible landed families on payment of a certain sum of money to the Exchequer.

Shortly after her marriage, Lady Anne Hawksworth became pregnant; but she was so frightened and alarmed by her husband's teenage pastime of 'shooting off' pistols close to the house that she took herself off to another place and there, to everyone's surprise, gave birth to twins. Whether it was believed that the multiple birth was the direct result of all the gunshots, we do not know! Eighteen months later, Sir Walter and a group of companions were living it up by 'drinking and ranting at a strange rate' in part of the hall. The drunkenness led to a serious argument, insults were ex-changed, and the young Sir Walter persuaded a kinsman, another Hawksworth, to settle the dispute by a sword fight with a certain Mr Sherburne, who, it was said, 'was more outragious than the rest'. The silly affray which followed led to the mortal injury of Sherburne, who was 'carryed in, dyed presently'.

*Sir Walter Hawksworth (1678–1735),
the second baronet.*

The young Sir Walter Hawksworth was not a healthy man. He was a consumptive, and at the age of twenty-two he suffered a sad and premature death. He was buried in Guiseley Church (1683) where his gravestone is still to be seen. He left a widow, Lady Anne, and the twins, one of whom (the daughter) was to die in childhood, leaving only one surviving offspring, Walter Hawksworth, the second baronet (1678–1735). It is plain to see that the Hawksworths were becoming 'thin on the ground' by the late seventeenth century, the result of a combination of childhood mortality, small numbers of offspring and early deaths of both male and female adult family members. This ancient family was in danger of dying out. In fact, Sir Walter the second baronet was destined to be the last Hawksworth at the hall by direct male descent.

On the 11th February 1695, Sir Walter the second baronet married Judith Ayscough of Osgodby. At that date he was sixteen years of age, and so he appeared to be following his father's preference for settling down whilst very young. Judith Ayscough's younger sister Margaret was to marry Francis Fawkes of Farnley, and so the Ayscough family was the important link between the Hawksworths and the Fawkes, leading ultimately to an 'amalgamation' at the end of the eighteenth century.

The eldest of Sir Walter and Lady Judith's two surviving children, both daughters, was Frances Hawksworth, born in 1702. She married Thomas Ramsden of Crowstone in 1722, and their only son, Walter Ramsden, assumed the additional surname of Hawksworth after the death of his maternal grandfather Sir Walter in 1735. At this date the baronetcy became extinct, and has never been revived.

Walter Ramsden alias Hawksworth himself died prematurely in 1760, in his thirties. He had been unwell for some time, and was 'taking the cure' at Bath. An old memorandum in the Gaunt Papers reads: 'Mr Hawksworth dyed at Burton upon Trent on Sunday morning 12th October 1760 on his way from Bath. Jn Swaine was with him, he was brought to Wakefield in a hearse from Burton and from Wakefield to Guysley in a leased mourning coach to be buried at Guysley 16th October 1760'. A long list of individuals who were to be given gold 'mourning rings' at the funeral is headed by 'Mr Fawkes, Farnley'. Walter Ramsden Hawksworth's wife, Frances Hall, had died five years earlier in 1755.

The significance and importance of 'Mr Fawkes' in 1760 can be explained by the fact that he – Ayscough Fawkes, a bachelor – had been appointed a trustee by Walter Ramsden Hawksworth's will, which automatically made him guardian of Walter's fourteen year old orphaned son, Walter, born in 1746. The link between the Hawksworths and the Fawkes, already established through the Ayscoughs, was reinforced when the Farnley Fawkes took over the responsibility for the welfare of the orphaned child.

Ayscough Fawkes of Farnley died in 1771, to be succeeded by his younger brother, Francis 'Frank' Fawkes, the so-called 'blunt squire', who continued to look after the interests of his kinsman Walter Hawksworth, forty years his junior. As Frank Fawkes and his wife Christiana were childless, it is likely that the young Walter Hawksworth was regarded almost as a son. Certainly in his early life, Walter Hawksworth would have needed the support and guidance of his uncles Ayscough and Frank and aunt Christiana at Farnley.

Francis Fawkes, the last of the original Fawkes, died on the 17th July 1786, leaving his extensive estates in Wharfedale and elsewhere to his kinsman Walter Hawksworth *provided* that Walter would make Farnley Hall his principal residence and change his surname to Fawkes. This was done, and Walter Hawksworth left his ancestral home at Hawksworth to become Walter Fawkes, the new Squire of Farnley.

Hawksworth Hall

The complicated and confusing architectural features of Hawksworth Hall, the result of so much rethinking and tinkering across the centuries, present a real puzzle to the person who is attempting to piece together in a logical manner the accumulation of venerable masonry on its historic site. The south front alone offers a bewildering array of architectural tit-bits, ranging from early seventeenth century ornamental stone finials on the roof to a late eighteenth century bay window. Alterations abound, entrances have been juggled around and windows replaced or shifted to alternative locations within the fabric.

The key to understanding the building's evolution lies in the roofspace. In March 1978, Colum Giles of the Royal Commission on Historical Monuments clambered into the loft of Hawksworth Hall to examine the roof timbers. Using his extensive knowledge of traditional timber construction, Mr Giles was soon able to show the way in which the house had expanded and evolved over two centuries. At least four phases of building development were identified.

The earliest portion, Mr Giles suggested, appeared to have been completed in the early seventeenth century. The most notable feature of this part of the house is the very imposing first-floor ceiling. The plasterwork bears the date 1611 and the coat of arms of Walter Hawksworth and his wife Isabel Colthurst, who we presume must have commissioned the building of this oldest-surviving part of the hall.

Modelled in plaster on the western wall of the same first-floor chamber is a royal coat of arms – that of King James I. This special feature has led to the room becoming known as the King's Chamber, although Harry Speight, writing around the turn of the century, could find no evidence to suggest that James or any other king actually slept here. In fact, this first floor room was likely to have been a grand parlour – a day sitting-room rather than a bedroom – providing pleasant south-facing long-distant views across the valley.

The 1611 portion of Hawksworth Hall now forms the western part of the present long building range. It is possible that this early

The coved plasterwork ceiling of the King's Chamber, Hawksworth Hall.

portion may contain stonework from an earlier building, but evidence for this is slight, and the wooden supporting structure for the 1611 coved plaster ceiling certainly appears to be an integral part of the building's original construction and not just a modification or addition.

A detailed inventory made immediately after the death of Sir Richard Hawksworth (1657) lists twenty-eight rooms as being part of this oldest house, although some of the rooms named must have been in outbuildings or in a part now long demolished. In 1657 the ground floor included a large hall, a dining parlour, a buttery, a low nursery, the kitchen, the dairy, the pastry, the 'backha' house, the larder, the brewhouse and a cellar. Of the first floor apartments, the 'great chamber' appeared to be the most important and best-furnished, including among other things four arm chairs, sixteen high stools, four low stools with embroidered work and two carpets. In all probability the 'great chamber' was the room nowadays called the King's Chamber.

Hawksworth Hall entered a second stage of evolution in the 1660s, when the house doubled in size by a major extension to the east. This development did much to increase the imposing character of the south front. The twin gables at the extreme east end were doubtless intended to 'balance' the original early seventeenth century ones at the west end of the facade. There is ample evidence surviving in the form of datestones to indicate that all this major building and extension must have taken place between 1660 and 1670. It was instigated by Walter Hawksworth and his wife Alice (nee Brownlow) who had succeeded Sir Richard Hawksworth at the family seat after 1657.

The outbuildings behind the hall appeared to be the first to receive attention from Walter and Alice. A completely new large barn, the external stonework of which still survives, was erected in 1661. By 1664 most of the construction of the eastern extension was complete – this date can be seen on a chimney stack. The well-known York glass artist, Henry Giles, was commissioned to supply the house with ornamental armorial glasswork. This was installed and dated 1666. The hearth tax roll of 1672 shows that the greatly-expanded Hawksworth Hall now had seventeen hearths.

It is the east wing of the hall which contains the mysterious hiding chamber or 'priest hole'. This can be reached by descending through the floor in the attic. The 'hole' is about five feet square by five feet high and is contained in the stonework beside the chimney stack dated 1664 previously mentioned. Access into the secret chamber is by way of a series of ledges in the stonework, forming rough steps. The hide exists behind a panelled chimney breast, but the panelling is backed by a stone wall, supposedly to thwart any attempt to discover the hide by tapping the panelling by the fireplace.

If this hidden cavity really was a hide, then it cannot have been a priest hole as the building is of too late a date. It is even too late to have been constructed during the Civil War period, when Sir Richard Hawksworth – who was a misfit among many of the local gentry because of his Parliamentary sympathies – might have felt the need for such a hide hole on sundry difficult days. There is really no certainty at all whether the feature in question was ever built as a hiding place: it might have been simply a bit of spare 'left over' space if a chimney and hearth replaced an earlier open firehood in 1664.

The third architectural development at the hall took place in the second quarter of the eighteenth century, when a dozen or so of the windows in the south front were replaced with new Georgian ones with moulded stone surrounds and raised keystones. These windows bear a strong stylistic resemblance to those at Low Hall,

Hawksworth Hall; the south front.

Menston (circa 1744, John Rhodes). The fourth architectural phase took place later in the eighteenth century, when the south-west front of the original 1611 house was totally remodelled to feature a new two storey bay window. A large dining room was created immediately behind the ground floor bay, decorated with the most fashionable features of the day, including a pair of very refined Grecian columns in the north internal wall.

One unsolved puzzle connected with the hall is the exact position of its former medieval chapel. The chapel is first recorded as early as 1343 (see Appendix 1) when Walter of Hawksworth was granted a licence by the Archbishop of York to hold 'divine service lawfully celebrated by a suitable chaplain' within its walls. Mention of the chapel occurs again over 200 years later, when the chapel and chapel chamber were two of a number of rooms in or near the house entitled to be occupied and used by Jane, the widow of Walter Hawksworth who was killed at the battle of Musselbrough (1547). Over a century later, Sir Richard Hawksworth's inventory at the time of his death in 1657 refers at least to a 'chapel chamber', containing one truckle bed, one livery cupboard, a long seat, two bolsters, two blankets and a rug.

A watercolour painting of Hawksworth Hall, done around the year 1768 by a William Daw or Dale, shows a large pointed Gothic window right in the middle of the south front, in that part of the house now the entrance hall. We can surmise that the window shown was certainly once a chapel window, but was it in its original position? Many existing medieval chapels are built on an east-west axis. The position of the Gothic window, facing south, seems unusual if not irregular.

There is some circumstantial evidence to suggest that the chapel might have stood a little way to the east of the 1611 hall. When the house was extended eastwards during the major extensions of the mid-1660s, the chapel may have been demolished and its best architectural feature – the window – re-used to form a feature on the south front. Henry Giles' armorial painted glass was delivered to the hall from the Giles workshops at York in 1666 at the time of the alterations. It is likely that the old Gothic window frame was thought to be the best receptacle for the new glass, especially as the theme of Giles' painting commemorated the Hawksworth family's long-established local standing.

When the Hawksworths moved to Farnley in the late eighteenth century, the glass followed them, to be installed in part of Farnley Hall. Then at the time of the mid nineteenth century Gothic revival and the restoration of Farnley church, the bits of painted glass were uprooted yet again and placed in the east window of the church, where they remain to this day. The pointed Gothic stone window frame had vanished from the south front of Hawksworth Hall by the early nineteenth century.

Another possible survivor from the former chapel at Hawksworth is the bell, which now functions on the wall of a private house five miles away. The bell in question used to be housed in a specially-constructed turret, positioned at the west gable end of a now demolished outbuilding to the rear of Hawksworth Hall. This outbuilding was certainly not of medieval date; but the bell, turret and building were photographed in 1898 by Robert Hawkesworth on a visit from his home at East Orange, New Jersey, USA, and a reproduction of the original print appears in this account. Further specialised investigation will be needed to determine whether the surviving bell is medieval or not.

The road between Hawksworth village and Guiseley passes in

Outbuildings to the rear of Hawksworth Hall, photographed circa 1898 by Robert Wright Hawkesworth of New Jersey, USA. The building on the left, with the gable-end bell turret, is now demolished.

front of the hall and divides the house and gardens from the large expanse of parkland (about seventy-two acres) formerly known as Hall Croft – now the golf course. Hall Croft was in existence in its present form by the late eighteenth century, being created at some unknown earlier date by the amalgamation of a number of smaller fields. The croft contains two wells – the Birkhill Well towards the west and the Tofts Well in the east part.

In 1769, Walter Hawksworth commissioned Thomas White (circa 1736–1811), an understudy of Capability Brown's, to draw up plans to landscape the croft and remove the highway from the front of the house and divert it over the hillside to the north of the outbuildings behind the hall. White's plans also included the removal of the old kitchen garden from its site at the top of the croft, immediately in front of the house, to a new out-of-sight location next to the village. The purpose of these proposed alterations was to provide Walter Hawksworth with a private and uninterrupted view of newly landscaped parkland.

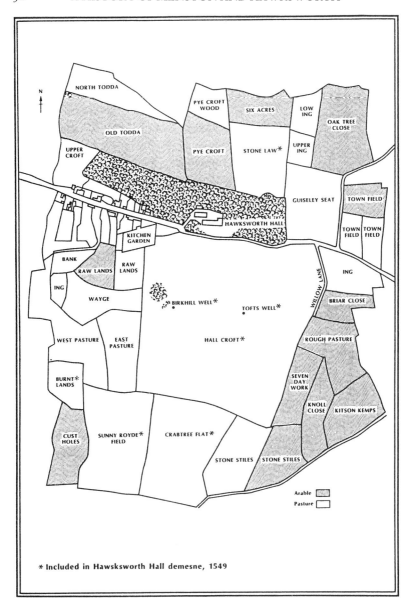

Hawksworth Hall, the village, and surrounding fields in 1811, showing land use.

Although the kitchen garden was indeed removed to its present position, the old right of way stuck to its original alignment, possibly because of objections from the local residents, who were put off by the thought of additional toiling up and down any new, steep, re-routed lane in order to gratify the Hawksworth whims. The old road survived, but it was made to sink into a hollow which hid it and its users from the leisurely elegance of the private apartments up above at the house.

Throughout the nineteenth century, the hall was let by the absentee Hawksworths, now living at Farnley, to a variety of tenants. Joseph Wilkinson, a distant relative, lived here until his death in 1810. He and his wife are buried in Guiseley Church. By 1822 the resident tenant was George Carroll, about whom nothing is known. Then in 1830 the house was let to Timothy Horsfall, a wealthy merchant and local magistrate who came from Bingley. Horsfall, who owned Norcroft farm at Hawksworth, lived in the village for almost fifty years. After his death in 1877 he was succeeded at the hall by his son, Thomas Moss Horsfall, who remained for a few years. From 1892 to 1899 the house was occupied by a Mr Reid, a Leeds businessman.

In 1899, Hawksworth Hall was let for a period of fifteen years to Duncan Law. By this time, the house and outbuildings, like many others in the village, had fallen into disrepair, and Mr Law had to undertake extensive repairs and alterations during the time he was tenant. When the Hawksworth estate came up for auction in 1919, the hall was not included in the auction sale – it was sold privately for the sum of £9,000 to the sitting tenant, Duncan Law, together with the surrounding gardens, paddocks, walled kitchen garden and woodland, in all comprising some twenty-seven acres. The Laws were to remain for only a further four years. In 1923 the property was purchased by Edgar L Gaunt, a leading Yorkshire textile manufacturer. It was some time after this date that a large collection of ancient Hawksworth archives – many of them dating back to the Middle Ages – were given to the Gaunt family by F H Fawkes. These surviving papers have proved very helpful in furnishing valuable information for this book; and the writer is grateful for the late David Gaunt's help in this connection.

The Gaunts were the last family to use the hall as a private dwelling. When the property came up for sale in 1955, it was purchased by the Bradford and District Spastics Society, who saw its great potential as a specialist residential school for handicapped children. It is pleasing to note that the school's improvements and extensions of recent years have been done in such a way as to retain the unique and special features of the old home of the Hawks-worths.

Hawksworth village

Touring motorists who chance upon the main street of Hawks-worth in the course of their cross-country travels are often surprised and delighted by the strong and unspoilt historic character of the village; but they are of course travelling far too quickly to take in any of the richness of detailed offered; and although Hawksworth is certainly well-known as a local beauty spot, very little in-depth investigation has yet been made into the village's long and fascinating evolution.

Within the walls of at least two of the houses in the village there exist bits and pieces of timber construction which are the relics of a former generation of timber homes – probably of medieval date. However, the bulk of the fabric of the old part of the village as we see it today appears to date from a period spanning the late seventeenth century and early eighteenth century. In spite of numerous superficial alterations to the appearance of these buildings by such things as porches and new windows etc, it is nevertheless possible to pinpoint a period during which a large amount of house building or rebuilding must have taken place, and during which time the layout of the village crystalised into its present form.

The period in question largely coincided with the time during which Hawksworth was ruled by Sir Walter Hawksworth the second baronet (1678–1735), and his wife Judith Ayscough (died 1724), the eldest daughter of John Ayscough of Osgodby. The historian Ralph Thoresby visited the Hawksworths in the summer of 1702 and noted in his diary:

'We dined with the ingenious Sir Walter Hawksworth, who is making pleasant alterations and additions to that ancient seat, and gardens etc; he entertained us agreeably with Roman histories & etc, wherein he is well versed, and accompanied us several miles in his own demesnes; inter alia he showed us a monumental heap of stones, in memory of three Scotch boys slain there by light-ning- - - -'.

Among the 'improvements' which Thoresby might have viewed were the new houses in the main street, which may not have been completely new houses as much as neatly and carefully modernised and restructured older, possibly timber-framed, edifices. In con-trast, the second half of the eighteenth century was a time of very little change in the village. After the Hawksworths left the hall shortly after 1786 to live at Farnley, alterations to the village remained few and far between. In fact, throughout the nineteenth century, so little change happened that the appearance of Hawksworth became 'fossilised' and the essentially early eighteenth century village character was preserved almost intact right through into the present century.

By 1900, the antique homes and farm buildings had dilapidated into a poor condition. This was doubtless the result of the agricultural depression of the late nineteenth century, which impoverished the small tenant farmer, prevented landlords from increasing rents and reduced the amount of spare capital available to improve agricultural homes and outbuildings. When the Bradford estate agents and surveyors Hollis and Webb undertook a survey and valuation of the Hawksworth Estate for F H Fawkes in 1900 (see Appendix 7), the 'very modest' rents were noted, but the condition of all the buildings in the village was a matter of some concern, and Hollis and Webb urged Mr Fawkes to immediately outlay the sum of £500 on re-pointing and other work to improve the overall condition of the village fabric.

It appears that it was originally the intention of F H Fawkes to sell by auction the entire estate at Hawksworth – hall, farms, cottages, woodland and moorland – as one complete entity to a single purchaser. To this end, a sale map was drawn up in 1901. For some reason there was a change of plan. The sale did not proceed and the Farnley Estate retained ownership for a further eighteen years. Then at the end of the First World War a decision was finally made to dispose of the ancestral homelands of the Hawksworths. In July 1919 the village was sold off, not to a single purchaser but by a series of twenty auction lots. Some of the new purchasers were to become owner-occupiers, and it was doubtless their appreciation of the merits of the characterful old buildings which had led them to purchase in the first place, and which further led them to conserve and repair rather than to demolish and build anew.

On entering the village from the low end, the first structure which comes to view is the large walled kitchen garden to the left, now aptly used as a nursery garden centre. Of a curious parallelogram shape (not always evident from the ground but discernible on a map) the kitchen garden is believed to date from the mid-eighteenth century, and was probably the work of Thomas White, the landscape architect who had been commissioned to remodel the old Hall Croft in 1769. Before this date, the original kitchen garden had been immediately in front of the hall, at the top end of the present golf course. Once the old walled garden had been moved nearer the village (possibly involving the demolition of a house or two in the process), then there was scope for transforming the ancient Hall Croft enclosure into a large area of informal parkland.

The well-constructed seventeenth century house which next follows the kitchen garden on the same side of the road – now divided into two homes called Squirrel Cottage and Wayside – was the homestead for one of the three principal farming tenants at Hawksworth. The farm was in fact known as Lunds, the fields of which lay some way to the south of the village and were reached by a cart track known as Willow Lane, still a pedestrian right of way through the golf course. The family who lived at the house during the early nineteenth century, the Shackletons, were noted for their longevity. Christopher Shackleton died in 1859 aged eighty-nine; and Robert Shackleton, presumably his brother, died in 1867 also aged eighty-nine.

At some date in the nineteenth century a new Lunds Farm was erected at the bottom of Willow Lane, much closer to the original fields, and the older house in the village street appeared to become redundant as a farmhouse. Adjoining the old house is Dean Mews, a row of modern houses which have been created in period style by converting an original farm building. The name 'Dean' in this case presumably comes from an old Hawksworth farming family resident at New Todda Farm (now called Hall Croft) during the last century.

Opposite Squirrel Cottage and Wayside, on the north side of the street, is a tall house now called Cherry Fold aligned at right angles to the road. This was once two dwellings, in one of which lived a certain Isaac Brown at the beginning of the nineteenth century. We believe that this person may have been one and the same as the Isaac Brown who was well-known as an early Methodist minister, being superintendant of the 'Haworth Round' of itinerant evangelical preachers. The elegant stone bay window on the east side of the house is of seventeenth century date, but of modern importation from some now-demolished gentry building. Its presence here certainly helps to confuse the architect historian's attempt to determine the true age of the house.

Further up the south side of the street is Manor House, positioned at a curious and awkward angle to the road. The building has been known as Manor House for at least the past ninety years. However, as the building is of late seventeenth or early eighteenth century date, and as the manor house for Hawksworth was always presumably the much older hall, then it is something of a puzzle to understand how this building was given its present name. Its earlier name was Stone Law Farm, and it was the second of the three principal farms in the village. Its fields lay immediately to the north of Hawksworth Hall, and included enclosures named as Stone Law, Pye Croft and Oak Tree Close. (For the location of these and other closes, see the accompanying map.) Possibly the close proximity of these fields to the hall, plus the fact that Stone Law was once part of the hall demesne in the sixteenth century, may have led to the name Manor Farm being given to the house in question.

The third of the three principal village farms, Sunny Royd, which stood immediately to the east of the present school, is now demolished. For most of the nineteenth century, Sunny Royd was the home of the Naylor family, leading local Methodists, and joiners and carpenters as well as farmers. The fields farmed by the Naylors were, like those of Lunds farm, some way to the south of the village and included some of the best soils in the township. Sunny Royd should not be confused with Sunny Side which still lies on the western edge of the village.

Hawksworth School was erected in 1875. It is one of the few buildings of nineteenth-century date in the village. As the initials of Ayscough Fawkes are carved with the date above the entrance porch, we can assume that Mr Fawkes must have provided the site for the school and also paid the construction costs. He had recently sold most of his Menston property, and so some spare finance would have been available for the school project. The present building replaces an earlier school run by the Rennard family, situated further up the village street. Marmaduke Rennard (born circa 1790) was running the village academy in 1822, having originally hailed from Baildon. He augmented his modest salary by taking in 'boarders', and according to the census return of 1851 the schoolhouse of the Rennards was occupied by five such children: William Foster (age 11), Joe Foster (8), William Holmes (10), Benjamin Shackleton (9) and Robert Shackleton (7). Marmaduke was assisted in his work by one of his sons, John, also described as a schoolteacher in 1851.

The Rennards were leading members of the Hawksworth community for most of the nineteenth century and into the twentieth. Like most Hawksworth residents, the family were Methodists and doubtless helped to establish the original chapel off Odda Lane in 1832. Marmaduke Rennard's son, Robert, laid

one of the foundation stones of the new and present chapel on the
12th July 1902. Robert's brother, Ambrose, died in 1919 at the
very advanced age of ninety-seven. He was probably the last of his
family to live at Hawksworth. The family moved down to
Guiseley. One of their number, the late Miss Kitty Rennard, a
diminutive but sprightly lady, was well-known in Guiseley for
three-quarters of the present century.

The old smithy and blacksmith's house in Hawksworth is now
called Cobblestones, the original lean-to smithy having been
modified, raised a storey and incorporated into the present house.
For many years this building was associated with the Mawson
family, who, as well as being blacksmiths, were sometime
landlords of the next-door public house, the Brown Cow. The
Mawsons can be traced back in Hawksworth to the mid-eighteenth
century. William Mawson was the blacksmith in the early decades
of the nineteenth, and by 1851 James Mawson was at the smithy.
The family were still resident at Hawksworth in the 1880s, in the
shape of Elizabeth Mawson, a widow.

Running close to the left side of Cobblestones and the former
smithy is the footpath which ascends up to the Odda and on to
Menston. This right of way appears to be the one referred to in a
series of disputes which arose in the early 1700s. At that time,
William Cliffe, a local resident, confirmed 'that his father hath
severall times told him that there was a way thro' in Atkinson's
house thorough the thro' entry there from the Towngate of
Hawksworth to the Warren called Todday and that he hath gone
that way without disturbance and without being asked why he
went that way, And says there's a way up at the west end of the
house'. Further evidence and information was supplied by Joseph
Padgett of Hawksworth, who 'sayth that he is above fifty years of
age and hath severall times since he came to years of Discretion
gone thorough to and fro betwixt the Towngate of Hawksworth
and the Warren, through a thorough entry in the house which now
belongs to Henry Atkinson and never was disturbed for goeing that
way, for which reason he believes there may be a way there and as
a reason to induce him to believe it he hath heard one Wm Holms
angery about that way and say that there was a way thru'. (The
documents concerning this footway now form part of the Gaunt
Papers.)

On the other side of the footpath in question is the house called
Hawkslyn. This building was none other than the Brown Cow
public house, occupied in the early 1800s by the Leach family,
although we do not know whether the building was actually in use

as an alehouse at this date. By 1822, William Mawson, the blacksmith, had become the victualler here. Like Cobblestones and most of the older houses in the village, Hawkslyn appears to be of late seventeenth or early eighteenth century construction. The story of how the Brown Cow closed its doors for the last time is well known. The landlord was forced to do so as a result of a local referendum, held because of complaints from the Methodist village community. Whether the complaints arose because of the rowdy antics of drunken revellers, or because there was concern about some of the locals spending too much time and money in the alehouse, we do not know. Possibly it was a combination of both. When the alehouse closed down around 1890, something of an unaccustomed hush must have descended on Hawksworth's nightlife.

Overlooking the junction of the main street with Odda Lane is the single storey cottage with modern extensions, known as Windyridge. The original name of this property was Ellis Croft. During the early part of the present century, the cottage was tenanted by the novelist William Riley, one of whose books, *Windyridge* (1912), was a best-seller in its day. The individuals portrayed in the novel were locally believed to have been based on a number of the 'characters' found at Hawksworth, but this claim was always denied by Riley himself. When the village of Hawksworth was sold off in 1919, Windryridge (by then a well-known building) was purchased at auction by a Mrs Clarke for £400. On the low side of the junction, immediately below the Riley home, is Sunnyside Farm, believed to have been the residence of the long-established Mitton family throughout the seventeenth and eighteenth centuries.

The old Methodist graveyard above Odda Lane is well worth a visit. The main gate, stone steps and straight path here led directly up to the old chapel (1832) demolished early this century. The way in which the tombstones form shelves on the steep hillside help to create a dramatic and special atmosphere at this spot. Most of Hawksworth's nineteenth century farming community are buried at this special place – the Popplewells, Naylors, Rennards, Tennants, Shackletons, Rhodes, Daveys and so forth. The present Methodist chapel, which replaced the old one at the head of the graveyard, has foundation stones all dated the 12th July 1902 and laid by 'Mr R. Rennard, Mr S. Jennings, Mr C. Holmes, Miss Law, Mr T. Rhodes, Mrs Cole, Mrs T. Turnbull, Messrs J. Warner and J. Wood on behalf of the local preachers, Mr J. Huddlestone and Mrs E. Watkinson'.

In concluding this brief tour round the village, we must not overlook one notable characteristic to be found in many of the local farm names: the use of the word 'side' as an ingredient in the name; and so we have Reva Side and Todday Side (both demolished farmsteads) and the existing Intake Side, Sunny Side, Hill Side, Spring Side and Lane Side. No other local townships offer such a repetitive use of this particular feature, and we wonder why it is peculiar to Hawksworth. The name is far more commonly found higher up the Dales (Whernside, Abbotside, Gunnerside etc) and it is particularly associated with settlements of Scandinavian origin – the word 'side' deriving from the Old Norse *saetr*, meaning 'hill pasture'.

The Odda

The prominent spur of bald, rounded hillside which provides some protection from northerly winds for the inhabitants of Hawksworth, and which hides their village from any prospect to the north or east, is called Odda; and the oddity of its name stems from the fact that it would appear to be a fairly modern concoction, the work perhaps of a nineteenth century map maker who was misled into believing that the original name 'Todda' was a local dialect pronunciation of 'the Odda'. All the documentary evidence prior to the nineteenth century suggests that this was not the case, and that the hill's true name should always have been 'Todda'.

A very detailed survey map of Hawksworth done in 1811 shows that the local farmers were able to distinguish at least four species of Todda: Old Todda, North Todda, New Todda and Near Todda. The various names describe the location and age of enclosures situated on the hill. It can be appreciated that it would have been illogical to think of such enclosures as 'Old the Odda' or 'New the Odda' and so forth.

In January 1722, one William Nicholson of Tranmire, aged eighty years, confirmed that he 'hath known the Towne of Hawksworth and a piece of ground called Todda thereto belonging for the spate of three score and ten years last past'. In December 1646, William Rhodes of 'Todday Side' made his will and implored his daughter Isobel 'to come to her mother and live with her as a Dutiful Child ought to doe'.

The earliest occurrence of the place name to be found at present is a charter of 1322, in which Hugh, son of Robert le Rous of Todhaw granted a capital messuage and six acres of land in Hawksworth to Thomas, son of Simon de Hawksworth.

If the landmark's original name was indeed 'Todhaw', then things begin to seem less odd and more logical, for *tod* is Old English for fox, and *haw* or *how* is also Old English for a spur-shaped hill. The nineteenth century cartographer who perhaps became a little confused on the Fox Hill cannot have been helped by the fact that the local farmers he met would have been surnamed Oddy and Todd!

The Reservoirs

Hawksworth has two reservoirs. The first is known as the New Dam, situated quite close to Hillings Lane midway between Burley Woodhead and Baildon. An estate survey map dated 1811 shows no reservoir existing in the township, other than a small mill dam to the south of Goose Lane; but by the time of the tithe award map (1849), New Dam had been constructed. Its original function appears to have been to conserve the waters of Jum Beck in order to improve the supply of water power for the millwheel at Hawksworth corn mill, half a mile to the south.

A second and much larger dam – Reva Reservoir – lies near the Bingley road some distance north-west of New Dam. Reva Reservoir was constructed shortly after 1889 by the Yeadon Waterworks Company, who had been given legal powers under the terms of the Parliamentary Yeadon Water Act to compulsorily purchase land at Hawksworth to 'divert, collect, impound and appropriate' the flow of water from Black Beck and Middle Beck, running off Hawksworth Moor. The land for the reservoir site was bought from Ayscough Fawkes of Farnley for the sum of £2,400 on condition that 'no beershop be allowed on the ground' and that 'no picnics of a public character' would be permitted. The directors of the Yeadon Waterworks Company were granted the special privilege of fishing and boating on their new reservoir: the ordinary townsfolk of Yeadon were quite content simply to receive a greatly-improved water supply through their taps.

Chapel Croft

On the borders of Hawksworth and Menston, tucked away in a belt of lonely and little-known countryside, sits Chapel Croft. This name, which is recorded as early as 1273 in a deed mentioning the boundaries of the two townships (see Appendix 3), evokes images of a solitary and curious sanctuary, inexplicably isolated from the main centres of village population, yet strategically placed on the township boundary.

The ruins of Chapel Croft farmhouse, 1989.

However, we are not even sure if a chapel existed here – on reflection, it seems unlikely. A rent payment for these 'Chapel Croft' fields may have simply provided an income for a local priest or curate. Possible links with Esholt Priory suggest themselves – we know that the prioress and her convent were given lands at nearby High Rhodes and Norcroft. The licence granted by Archbishop William Zouche to Walter Hawksworth in 1343 to hold 'divine service lawfully celebrated by a suitable chaplain in the excellent chapel situated within your manor of Hawksworth' (see Appendix 1) is likely to refer to the private chapel within the walls of the old Hall at Hawksworth, the existence of which is known for certain.

Whatever the truth behind the origin of the name is, we do know that Chapel Croft was in fact a small farm, that it was home for a branch of the ubiquitous Rhodes family throughout the seventeenth century, and that part of the farm remained in the hands of the Rhodes' descendants until 1815. In 1636, William Rhodes of High Rhodes granted to his younger brother Christopher a house and a close of land (among others) called Chapel Croft Ing; and a certain Nicholas Rhodes of 'Chappellcroft within the Townshipp of Hawkesworth' made his will on the 8th June 1641. By the mid-eighteenth century, Chapel Croft formed part of the land holdings of Gregory Rhodes and the Nichols family of Norcroft. An auction sale map dated the 2nd September 1874 (Dacre and Son) shows High Chapel Croft and Low Chapel Croft to be among the fields offered under lot twenty-one.

Much speculation surrounds the age, origin and function of the stone-vaulted underground chamber which still remains at Chapel Croft. It is certainly not a 'secret passage', nor is it any kind of ecclesiastical edifice. It is a down-to-earth farmhouse cellar, a food store built at the east side of the now ruinous Chapel Croft farmhouse.

Nichols and Mittons

A history of Hawksworth would not be complete without some mention of two families who once played a leading role in local affairs, but who are now completely forgotten. They were the Nichols and the Mittons. Both families were of independent yeoman status – they farmed their own lands and remained outside the control of local squirearchy for many generations. Neither family was totally dependent on farming, however. The Mittons were weavers of serge and linen, and the Nichols were tanners and wheelwrights.

The home of the Nichols for a period spanning over 200 years was the now-isolated farm called Norcroft on the borders of Hawksworth and Menston. In former ages, Norcroft was far less remote than it appears today, as there were three or four other small farms in close proximity, the buildings of which have largely disappeared. The now demolished farmhouse at Norcroft had the date 1671 inscribed on the stone lintel above the door, although the Nichols themselves were here from at least the early seventeenth century.

One of their number, John Nichols, became puritan minister of Thornton Chapel, Bradford, during the mid-seventeenth century. Nichols was noted in his day as being an excellent preacher and orator, but his fondness for heavy drinking and loose company gave him a dubious reputation. According to a contemporary, Oliver Heywood, Nichols would have said to his flock 'You must not heed me but when I am got three foot above the ground', meaning into the pulpit. An Otley church memoranda of 1654 refers to a pew within the parish church there belonging to 'Mr Nichols, preacher at Thornton, for his lands at Norcroft'.

The sixty acre farm site at Norcroft can be dated back as early as 1262. It may well have been in existence as a settlement long before this early date, and its chief topographical features include an interesting plateau of higher land (the site of the original 'north croft') immediately behind the farm buildings, as well as ancient farm boundaries clearly defined by small rivulets and streams.

We know that by 1262 Nicholas Warde had given Norcroft to the Priory of Esholt, but we do not know how the farm came into the hands of the Nichols at a much later date. The fields on the farm in 1808 were called: the Croft Hill, Middle Ground, Limestone Close, Middle Ing, Upper Ing, Lyne Acre, Cattle Ing, Crabtree Ground, Little Ing, Dicky Ing, Near Croft, Sir Walter's Close, the three Chapel Crofts, New Intake and Dicky Intake. The fields named 'Dicky' may well be so-named from Richard Nichols, a leading member of the family here between circa 1678 and 1739. Richard's mother was Isobel Rhodes, a member of the well-established Rhodes clan.

On the 7th October 1808 the family continuity at Norcroft came to an end when Elizabeth Nichols of Idle (widow of Abraham Nichols) and her three sons, Francis of Newall, Otley, Abraham of Otley and Samuel of the City of York, sold their ancestral home to John Todd of Hawksworth.

The surname Mitton is a very uncommon one in this part of Yorkshire. The name derives from the obscure village of Mitton on the old borders of Yorkshire and Lancashire. As the Manor of Mitton once formed part of the estates of the Hawksworth family, we can suggest that the earliest local Mittons may have undertaken the trek from their native village as a result of some personal contact with a member of the Hawksworth family.

An interesting indenture dated the 16th April 1517 mentions that Thomas Hawksworth of Hawksworth 'haith solde and delyvered to William Forster and Agnes his wyff the wardship and custodie of the body of James Mitton son and heire of Christopher Mitton late of Hawkesworth, descessed, with the maredge profetts of all the landes and tenements of the seid James. To holde and to have the seid wardship, custodie, maredge, landes and tenementis to the seide William Forster and Agnes his wyff and to their assignes duryinge the noneage of the said James for the somme of 4 marks 11d'.

The young orphaned James Mitton must have survived his wardship and childhood days with the Forsters, for we find him listed in the 1539 muster of Hawksworth as 'Jamez Mytton', one of nine individuals in the village described thus: 'These be archers having no harnes, fotmen, abill persons'.

A Hawksworth rental roll of 1629 makes mention of 'James Mitton, his free rent, 11d'. Generation after generation of Mitton males were all given the same Christian name, James. On the 3rd May 1757, James Mitton the elder sold to his son James the younger the family farm at Hawksworth for the sum of £300. We believe that the location of the Mitton's home was Sunnyside Farm, a seventeenth century house on the edge of the village. It is known that the Mittons were cloth weavers, and the larger upper windows of Sunnyside farmhouse would suggest use as a weaving shop. The evidence for suggesting Sunnyside as the probable Mitton home is based on the fact that most of the fields named in the 1757 deed can be traced to this vicinity.

During the second half of the eighteenth century, some of the Mittons moved away from the village and settled at Trees in the parish of Fewston, where they continued their trade of cloth weaving. The senior branch, represented by James Mitton the younger and his only child, a daughter Elizabeth, eventually sold the ancestral property at Hawksworth to Walter Fawkes of Farnley. A junior branch, represented by Joseph Mitton, was based at Reva Side Farm (close to the present Reva Reservoir). Joseph had an illegitimate child, James, by a certain Miss Asquith. After Joseph's death, James Asquith changed his surname to Mitton and moved to Burley Woodhead, where he died in 1844 aged seventy-three, being as far as we know the last of the Mittons. Reva Side Farm, after passing through the hands of the Walker family, was sold to the Farnley Estate shortly before the purchase by Yeadon Waterworks of land for the reservoir.

High Rhodes alias High Royds

The surname Rhodes is one of the oldest local family names. There is evidence to show that a family bearing this surname lived in a woodland clearing (*rode* being an Old English word for clearing) from as early as the thirteenth century until the eighteenth, an impressive span of time. The clearing in question was sited above the village of Menston, at a higher altitude, and halfway along the old route to Hawksworth. The Rhodes family took their name from this clearing, which was always called High Rhodes until the 1880s, when, almost overnight, and for no obvious reason, the locality became known as High Royds.

Walter Ramsden Beaumont Hawksworth (1746–92) and his wife Amelia, née Farrar. After 1786 the couple were known as Walter and Amelia Fawkes.

Charles Fairfax of Menston (1597–1673).

In the mid-thirteenth century we find Simon 'de Rodes' living in Menston. His name appears in a charter (undated) which also names two of Simon's sons, William and Hugh. The charter concerns the release and 'quitclaim' of four acres of land in the 'Field of Rodes', which Simon had previously granted to his son William and which had been sold to Walter of Hawksworth. In 1281, Walter son of Walter of Hawksworth granted to the priory of Esholt land at Rhodes with a yearly rent of 4s 4d from Thomas son of Simon of Rhodes, 2s 6d from Robert Rufus and 15d from William son of Simon of Rhodes.

By the time of the poll tax of 1379, we find two householders, John of the Rhodes and Agnes of the Rhodes, each paying 4d in dues. The name 'John de Rodes' of Menston occurs in a deed dated the 10th May 1431. Members of the family soon spread out from their original habitat, and from the sixteenth century onwards we can trace branches living at Hawksworth, Esholt, Guiseley, Chevin End and Otley, all of which doubtless sprang from the same root at Menston.

Towards the end of the sixteenth century, the resident Rhodes at Rhodes was John, a yeoman, who married Isobel Breary, daughter of John Breary, gentleman, of Menston Old Hall. John Rhodes died in 1619 (his will being proved on the 30th September of that year), leaving a widow Isobel and no less than ten children: Isobel, William, Christopher, Jeffrey, Elizabeth, Richard, James, Margaret, Thomas and George. Of these brothers and sisters we do know a few details. Jeffrey (1599–1672) stayed on the family farm throughout his life, in all probability remaining a bachelor; Isobel married Anthony Ward; Elizabeth married Thomas Dunwell; George the youngest brother (born 1614) eventually became the sole owner of High Rhodes by the mid-seventeenth century – how or why we do not know, as the property had originally been inherited by the oldest brother William. On the 26th November 1670, George and Elizabeth his wife sold their family estate to an older brother Richard (1604–89), and High Rhodes was to remain in the hands of Richard's descendants until 1815.

Throughout the seventeenth century, the Rhodes remained leading members of the Menston community, their status being that of yeomen. Although most of the family appeared to be illiterate at this time, the fact that they were cousins of the Fairfaxes of Menston Old Hall (through marriage with the Brearys) meant that they were inevitably well-connected. One branch of the Rhodes – settling at Low Hall – were described as 'gentlemen' by the early 1700s.

High Rhodes, now called High Royds Hall.

The rugged and characterful three storey house which today stands at High Rhodes is the last surviving of a number of old homesteads in this vicinity. The house appears to date from the mid-seventeenth century, and we can guess that it might have been built for George and Elizabeth Rhodes. Unfortunately there is no trace of any dated or initialled stones on the house which might give a few clues to the local historian. A first floor doorway (now walled up) probably dates from the eighteenth century when the Exleys, as tenants of the Rhodes, were weaving cloth in a room of the house.

Richard Rhodes – who had bought High Rhodes from his brother and sister-in-law in 1670 – moved to Knaresborough. He and his wife Elizabeth were succeeded by their son David, a prosperous lawyer, and then by their grandson Gregory (1687–1766). There survives in the Gaunt Papers a letter from Gregory Rhodes to Walter Hawksworth dated the 11 March 1757, in which Gregory mentioned that he had been '5 weeks in the Gout, but now thank God on the recovery'. The letter referred to a 'very small piece of land' lying within High Rhodes Farm which

A watercolour painting of Hawksworth Hall by William Daw or Dale, circa 1768.

A watercolour painting of Menston Hospital, 1885, by Herbert Martin. The proposed Hospital church, shown in the left foreground, was never in fact constructed.

apparently belonged to Walter Hawksworth. Gregory was at a loss to explain how this had come about, but wrote, 'as the matter is very small, I leave my Self to your Candid and good disposition, as a friendship has so long subsisted in the Familey'. The long friendship alluded to had probably existed for some 400 years!

After their deaths, Gregory and his wife Eleanor were buried in a family vault in the chancel of Knaresborough Church. The lavish black marble tombstones which today still cover the vault suggest that the family were extremely affluent. Gregory and Eleanor had only one child, a daughter Ann, who married Robert Harper. Ann and Robert Harper in turn had only one child, a daughter Sarah, who married Daniel Wilson of Dallam Tower, Westmorland, in 1782. It was the Wilsons who sold their High Rhodes Estate on the 5th April 1815, so ending an incredibly long span of family continuity which can only be parallelled locally by that of the Hawksworths.

Between 1815 and 1874, High Rhodes and the neighbouring farm of High Ash belonged to the Cunliffe Lister family of Manningham Mills, Bradford. We assume that their purchase of the property was purely a financial investment, and that the Listers had no personal interest in their Menston lands. On the 2nd September 1874, the two farms were bought at auction by Ayscough Fawkes of Farnley Hall. At this date, Mr Fawkes was busy selling off his property in Menston village for housing development, and so the purchase of High Rhodes would appear to have been a logical means of consolidating the surviving scattered agricultural holdings of the Farnley Estate on the borders of Hawksworth and Menston; but Ayscough Fawkes' interest here was to last only eight years, for on the 11th September 1882, 287 acres of farmland, including High Rhodes, High Ash and Menston Moor End Farm, was sold for £17,240 to the West Riding County Council for the purpose of providing a site for a new 'pauper lunatic asylum'.

The individual who negotiated with Mr Fawkes for the purchase of the land was Francis Darwin (1825–1920) of Creskeld Hall, Arthington, a local magistrate. It was Mr Darwin who had persuaded the county justices to site their new asylum at Menston. He had organised a clandestine visit to the High Rhodes site (probably via the new railway station) by a party of county officials.

It is curious to learn that Francis Darwin's original surname was none other than Rhodes. He had assumed the additional surname Darwin on the occasion of his marriage to Charlotte Darwin in

1849. His father was William Rhodes of Bramhope; his grand-father was Peter Rhodes, a soap manufacturer of Leeds; and his more distant ancestors were the Rhodes of High Rhodes.

The Bleachworks

The former Rombaldsmoor Bleachworks was sited just outside Menston, in Burley Woodhead; but as the vehicle access to the works, as far as we know, was always from Menston village, the bleachworks had much closer ties with Menston than with Burley; and from the 1860s onwards a number of Menston residents were to find employment in the bleaching processes until the eventual closure of the premises in 1927.

The early history of the premises is still clouded in obscurity, and more detailed research remains to be done. We know that the existing bleachworks house (formerly home of the manager and his family) and the adjoining outbuildings had been erected by 1848 – probably not much before this date – but we do not know what the original industrial function of the building was. As the availability of plentiful water played an integral role, we assume that the early activities of the premises were textile, and that the building may have had some connection with the nearby Myrtle Grove Mill above the bleach mill site. John Padgett ran Myrtle Grove in the 1840s and 50s as a woollen mill. It is highly likely that he was the same Padgett who owned the bleachworks buildings as well, for the Gills who later came to Menston to bleach linen yarn are recorded as having bought their premises from a Mr Padgett.

There is no record in the 1851 census return of the existence of any bleaching activity locally; but the following census of 1861 shows that the Rombaldsmoor premises were in use, and that the resident bleachers were members of the Stott, Hancock, Teal, Ingleby and Wigglesworth families. Most of these individuals must have lived in the row of cottages which formerly stood near the bleach mill dam. Ten years later, the bleach mill had a resident manager, in the shape of James Mackinley, a Scotsman. Mackinley was still there in 1881, and by this date one of his sons, fifteen year old George, was the 'clerk at bleachworks' according to the census details of that year.

The firm which ran the premises from the 1870s until 1927 was known as Joseph Gill and Sons. Founded by Joseph Gill (1816–79), a linen yarn bleacher of Iveson House, Cookridge, Leeds, the company was active at the Headingley Bleachworks on the borders of Horsforth and Headingley. In 1874, Joseph Gill bought

Hagwood Farm at Menston, indicating that by this date the Gills already had an interest in the adjacent bleachworks. Shortly after the death of Joseph Gill in 1879, his second son William (born 1843) moved the whole business to the Rombaldsmoor site. William Gill, a bachelor, was succeeded by his nephew, Joseph Horsburgh Gill (born 1868), and the latter was in turn joined by his son Brian (born 1896), who represented the fourth Gill generation involved in the family business.

Up to the end of the First World War, Rombaldsmoor Bleachworks was engaged solely in the bleaching of linen yarn, which was manufactured at the mills in Leeds. Collection and delivery of the yarn was done on a door-to-door basis by horse and cart, and at one time the works stabled sixteen horses for this purpose. The works were quite conveniently sited for the local railway, and Menston Station became the delivery point for bulk items such as coal and chemicals for the bleaching process. Following a sharp decline in linen yarn manufacture after 1918, Joseph Gill and Sons turned to another kind of bleaching process – that of the treatment of cotton rag, which was supplied by a Dewsbury firm called Armitage. The rag was bleached white for recycling as cotton dusters.

During the 1920s, there was growing concern about the pollution of the watercourse – Dry Beck and Carr Beck – by waste products from Gill's works. Trout and other fish in the Wharfe at Burley were being killed by the leakage of toxic waste, and strong protests were made by local anglers. Growing opposition to the bleachwork's activities forced the Gills to consider a relocation, and a new site was found at Selby. In 1927 the works closed down and the Gill family, with their foreman George Reynolds and his family, left the district. The works became derelict, never to be used again for industrial purposes; and ultimately most of the buildings were dismantled and the large iron bleaching vessels scrapped. The work's manager's house and adjoining carthouse, an attractive group of buildings, still remain on the site.

Menston Grange

Situated at the 'Top of the Town' in Menston is a solidly-built farmhouse with the initials RHS and the date 1672 carved in stone above the porch door. The building is Menston Grange, now divided into two homes. For some time it was guessed among locals that the initials 'RHS' stood for 'Royal High Sheriff'; but research into the history of this house has turned up no evidence of

Menston Grange.

regality, nor even a sheriff. Nevertheless, this house was built for a Yorkshireman who was a very wealthy and high-ranking church official: he was Robert Hitch, Dean of York.

The Hitch link with Menston goes back to the first half of the seventeenth century, when Robert More, Rector of Guiseley, bought a farm in Menston from Jeffrey and William Pickard. Under the terms of Robert More's will, dated the 22nd July 1642, the farm was left to his son Timothy. Two years later Timothy More himself died, and the Menston farm was inherited by his younger sister Sarah, the wife of Robert Hitch. In 1672 the present Grange house was erected (possibly on the site of an older house of the Pickards) for Sarah and her husband Dean Hitch. By this date, the couple were elderly, and so the house here must have been regarded by them as a 'rural retreat' away from the busy administrative work at York. It is Robert's and Sarah's initials which remain proudly carved on the Grange porch to this day.

Robert Hitch began his local ecclesiastical career in 1627, when he was appointed Rector of Adel. On the death of his father-in-law

Robert More in 1644, Hitch succeeded him as Rector of Guiseley. After the restoration of the monarchy in 1660 and the renewed tolerance of 'pluralists' (churchmen who retained more than one 'living'), Hitch regained the Rectory of Adel, and in 1662 he was installed Archdeacon of the East Riding. On the 22nd December 1664, he was elected Dean of York.

We have somewhat conflicting reports about Robert Hitch's character. On the one hand it has been suggested that he was of a generous disposition, as evidenced by his will (1676) in which he gave certain property in Guiseley and Yeadon in trust to pay twenty shillings annually to the poor of Guiseley. However, as Hitch himself was reputedly worth £24,000 at the time of his death (if so, a vast fortune at that date), the setting up of this charity was not exactly a great sacrifice to himself or his family.

Canon Raine, describing some of the seventeenth-century ministers of York, declared that Hitch was a 'cold-hearted, penurious man, who had no sympathy with any one or any thing but his money bags'. Oliver Heywood, a contemporary of Hitch, had this to say of him: 'He was one of the richest churchmen in the country. He used to boast that for divinity, law and physic he would play with any man. A man of parts; he practised physic (medicine); was said to be in a consumption thirty years before he died'.

After the death of Dean Hitch in 1676, the family moved away from Menston. Henry Hitch, the only surviving son, moved to Leathley and established a three generation Hitch dynasty at Leathley Hall. Menston Grange and its lands were then occupied by tenants throughout the eighteenth century, such as David Rhodes (1746). When Menston Common was enclosed in 1773, Miss Ann Hitch of Leathley was entitled to quite a large slice of newly-enclosed land because of her ownership of the grange. She was the last member of her branch of the family. All her property at Leathley and Menston eventually passed to her niece, Anna Maria, the wife of James Maude of Gildersome; and it was the executors of Anna Maria Maude who disposed of their inherited Menston estate in the year 1797.

The purchaser of Menston Grange was a certain Griffith Wright of Harehills, Leeds. We discover that Mr Wright was a printer and publisher; he had founded a newspaper called the *Leeds Intelligencer* (forerunner of the *Yorkshire Post*) in 1754; we know that in 1797 he was aged about sixty-five; and we also know that in the same year he wrote and published *A History of Leeds*; but we do not know why he decided to buy the grange at Menston!

Griffith Wright was succeeded by his grandson, also called Griffith Wright (born 1784) of Harehills House, who continued to publish the *Leeds Intelligencer* until 1818 and who retained ownership of Menston Grange – as an absentee landlord – until his death in 1846. This Griffith Wright never married. His sister Frances, the wife of Ralph Markland, inherited her brother's grange, which she subsequently passed on to her son Bertie (1857). The Marklands then remained owners for the next forty years.

In 1874, Bertie Markland (then living at Harrogate) died, to be succeeded by his son, another Bertie Markland. On the 23rd November 1882, Bertie junior signed a tenancy agreement for the grange with a farmer called Christopher Lupton, who came from Denton. This event marked the beginning of the Lupton family's long association with the grange which has continued down to the present day.

The Luptons can be traced back to the hamlet of Starbotton, in upper Wharfedale. During the mid-nineteenth century the family moved down-valley to Denton, where they were farming nearly 300 acres on the Denton Hall Estate. It is not known why Christopher and his wife Grace decided to move to the smaller farm of Menston Grange; but as the couple were both in their mid-fifties by the time of the removal, they may have been seeking a more compact and easier to manage tenancy. The couple had a family of five: Elizabeth, Thomas, John, Christopher and Jane, whose ages ranged between about twenty-four and fifteen when the family settled in at the grange.

Thomas Lupton, the eldest son, married Catherine Mary Hearfield of Storris House Farm, Otley (once part of Menston Low Hall farm, now part of the golf course). The young couple took on a farm tenancy at Beamsley for some years. Back in Menston, the grange was put up for sale after the death of the last surviving member of the Markland family early in 1896. On the 13th July of that year, Thomas Lupton of Beamsley purchased the grange and surrounding farmland for the sum of £5,575. His parents remained in residence until their deaths in 1904. By this date, Thomas and Catherine had moved to Mount Pleasant Farm, Farnley, where their grandson James Lupton and his family now live.

The Lupton continuity at Grange Farm was maintained after 1904 in the shape of John Lupton, younger brother of Thomas of Farnley, who lived here with his wife Annie until 1923. In this year Thomas died, and his widow Catherine then moved across to the Grange for a few years before leaving for London to live with her daughters in 1926.

Thomas and Catherine Lupton. The original photograph is
unfortunately damaged.

The present day Grange Farm includes what was formerly known as Hagwood Farm adjoining to the west. Comprising of about sixty-four acres, this farm was for six centuries part of the Hawksworth family's holding in Menston village. (Le Hagge was in 1299 leased by a Walter Hawksworth.) Hagwood Farm was sold by Ayscough Fawkes to Joseph Gill of the nearby bleachworks in September 1874. In 1910, the Gills, who were then in a spot of financial trouble, had to dispose of the farm, and it was auctioned by Dacre and Son at the White Horse Hotel, Otley, on the 22nd April of that year. The purchaser again was Thomas Lupton; and the ancient Hagwood domain of the Hawksworths was amalgamated with the old grange lands of the Pickards, Mores, Hitches, Wrights, Marklands and Luptons.

Before taking leave of this part of Menston with its long and complicated history, we could reflect a little on the local significance of the name 'grange'. During the Middle Ages, a grange in Wharfedale or Airedale was synonymous with a monastic sheep farm, attached to an abbey, and occupied primarily with the growing of a wool 'crop' for export to Europe. A document of 1428 shows that the Abbot of Kirkstall held certain lands in Burley and Menston. About twenty acres of Menston Grange once spilt across the township boundary into Burley, and these particular fields (mainly the Foulscarrs) were part of the grange from at least the early eighteenth century, probably long before. Were the local Kirkstall Abbey lands based at Menston Grange? Further investigation will be needed to try and find out.

Derry Hill

According to a local tradition – a tradition which may not be many decades old – Derry Hill takes its name from the number of Irish labourers engaged in building and quarrying activities here during the nineteenth century. However, the census returns for Menston, 1841 to 1881, show little evidence of Irish families forming part of the local community. Moreover, a deed of 1797 (being a sale of former Hitch lands to Thomas Exley) includes reference to a field, once part of Menston Common, known as Derry Close Allotment. It would appear, therefore, that the place name is older than we may have been led to believe.

The Old English word *dwerry* means dwarf; and it was quite a common practice to name natural features such as hillocks and knolls after elfin or fairy folk. We could suggest that a possible Menston 'Dwerry Hill' might have been so named.

Searching through the earliest Menston deeds and charters for other possible clues, we stumble across the mention of a place in the village called Dowayngayl at the very early date of 1295. This isolated example of a curious and otherwise unrecorded name looks as though it could be an amalgamation of the Celtic *Dow*, meaning black, with the Old Norse *gill,* describing a steep and narrow valley. If we are so disposed, a stiff walk over the top of Derry Hill brings us to the narrow and steep-sided ravine called Matthew Dike, which forms the boundary division between Hawksworth and Menston. In 1273 this same dike or ravine was known as Black Syke (see Appendix 3). If Menston folk of former ages pointed up the hill and explained to the visitor that that was the way to Dowayn Gill, then it is easy to understand how the name of the hillside might have evolved into the modern rendition of Derry Hill.

On the right hand side of Derry Hill, going up, is a group of sloping fields, most of which were in former ages known as Tofts. The fields bearing various versions of this name extend as far as Hillings Lane on the west and Bingley Road to the south. Eighteenth century estate maps of Menston show an interesting variety of tofts in the vicinity: Low Tofts, High Tofts, Long Tofts, Sun Tofts, Rhodes Tofts and Wallace Tofts (the latter sometimes mistakenly called Wales Tofts because of mispronunciation of an archaic spelling of the local surname Wallace or Wallis).

The Tofts were certainly important lands in Menston at one time. Throughout the Middle Ages and onwards into the eighteenth century, most farmers had certain 'lands in the Tofts'. The fields here were enclosed and cultivated long before those on the other side of Derry Hill, which formed part of Menston Common until as late as 1773. The notable abundance of the 'Toft' field-name is a strong pointer to well-established Danish settlement at Menston. Two of the field names still survive today as house names in Moor Lane – Low Toft and High Toft.

Fairfax Hall or Menston Old Hall

Fairfax Hall is so named because of its association with the well-known family of that name who lived on this spot between circa 1625 and circa 1712, thereafter remaining absentee landlords until 1763. The present house appears to have been built in the mid-seventeenth century; but another house upon or near the same site was the home for Charles Fairfax's wife's family, the Brearys (or Brearhaughs), for many generations before.

Charles Fairfax (1597–1673) was the third son of Sir Thomas Fairfax of Denton. He and Mary Breary of Menston moved into Mary's ancestral home shortly after their marriage in 1625. Fairfax took the trouble to collect and write down much of the known genealogical information about the long-established Brearys. The facts are contained in his hand-written *Analecta Fairfaxiana*, a small notebook crammed full of minute ancestral details. One of two known copies of this valuable historical source, written in Charles Fairfax's own hand, can be found in the Brotherton Collection in Leeds University Library.

Fairfax had discovered that the Brearys could be traced back to the hamlet of Breary, near Bramhope, where they were living in the early thirteenth century. A branch of the family had settled at

A page from the manuscript Analecta Fairfaxiana *by Charles Fairfax, showing the arms of the Breary family of Menston.* (Reproduced by permission of the University of Leeds)

'Mensington' by the first half of the fourteenth century. Fairfax also realised that one of the fields on his wife's family farm – the Hallsteads – was quoted in a fourteenth century deed involving a certain Henry, son of Matilda of Mensington and William 'de Breraugh'. This same field still formed part of the Hall Farm in Fairfax's day. As most Menston residents will realise, the name survives today in the modern street Halstead Drive, the houses and gardens of which are sited within the boundary of the ancient enclosure.

It is likely that the Brearys succeeded the Mensington family as principal landowners in the village. Alexander Breary was described as one of the 'joint lords' (with the Hawksworths) of the manor in 1315. As the unusual Christian name Alexander (unusual, at least, in Yorkshire) was one used by the Mensingtons as well, we can suggest that a family connection existed. Alexander was followed by no less than ten further generations of Brearys, and we may assume that all of them must have lived in that part of Menston near the present Fairfax Hall.

William 'de Brehagh', son of Alexander, paid no more or less tax than his neighbours the Pickards and Rhodes (4d) in the poll tax of 1379. The various fields and enclosures attached to the Breary's Old Hall Farm were scattered somewhat haphazardly throughout the western end of the township. These included various enclosures in the Tofts, and a straggled chain of linked fields to the east of Burley Old Lane, including Hallsteads, Cow Close, and Rainey Croft.

At some date in the mid-sixteenth century, John Breary of Menston was married to Margaret Beckwith of Scow Hall, Norwood. She was the daughter and heiress of John Beckwith and a member of one of the distinguished 'Forest families' attached to the lands of the Duchy of Lancaster at Knaresborough Forest. This marriage and inheritance gave the Brearys land in Washburndale, and we find them bearing an elaborate coat of arms with quarterings by this period.

During the second half of the sixteenth century, John and Margaret Breary raised a large family of eleven children. Four of the boys, Stephen, Francis, Thomas and Walter, died in childhood. One daughter, Isobel, married John Rhodes of High Rhodes (see High Rhodes); another daughter Margaret married another John Rhodes of Menston (see Low Hall); and a third daughter Anne married William Fourness of Menston (see Kirklands). The eldest son and heir of this enormous family was John Breary junior, who was married to Elizabeth Morehouse; but he died in 1613, six years before his father, leaving only one surviving child, young Mary, who was to become the wife of Charles Fairfax. The intricate family connections can be better seen from the outline pedigree (see page 102) which shows that the Fairfax, Rhodes and Fourness families of Menston were all cousins during the seventeenth century.

It is for his work as an antiquarian and genealogist that Charles Fairfax of Menston is best known. His academic life was based at Trinity College, Cambridge, which he entered in 1611. He had legal training, and was called to the Bar at Lincoln's Inn on the 9th March 1618. The full extent of his involvement in the Civil War, twenty-five years later, is not known. It seems as though Fairfax was a reluctant soldier, certainly when compared with his nephew, the illustrious General 'Black Tom' Fairfax of Nun Appleton. He was also little interested in public office. Towards the end of the Commonwealth period, he was persuaded to take service as a colonel of foot, a position which he held in General Monck's army in Scotland at the time of the Restoration (1660). When Monck's army marched south into Yorkshire, Charles Fairfax was appointed Governor of the Port of Hull, an important position he seemed pleased to relinquish after about a year. Fairfax could not wait to return to the comfort of his studies, his books and the rural seclusion of Menston village.

There is one incident involving Menston which has entered many of the history books dealing with the Civil War period in Yorkshire. It concerns an important meeting which took place in the orchard of the Old Hall a few days before the battle of Marston Moor (the 2nd July 1644). Cromwell and other Parliamentary leaders were present on this warm summer's day, presumably to discuss and plan the tactics and strategy of the forthcoming warfare. Why this particular meeting took place at Menston, we do not know; nor do we know why this particular conference was recorded for posterity when many other similar ones remain unremembered. The small rectangular stone table around which the Parliamentary leaders sat in the orchard of the Old Hall soon became regarded as an important Civil War relic. In 1814 it was removed to Farnley to form an integral part of a collection of Cromwelliana and Civil War memorabilia at Farnley Hall.

Menston Old Hall underwent a major reconstruction during the 1650s. The earlier house of the Brearys was either demolished completely or incorporated into part of the new fabric, the main feature of which was a couple of wing extensions, lying parallel and quite close together, projecting southwards towards the

The stone Cromwell table, formerly situated in the orchard of Menston Old Hall.

courtyard. Each wing appeared to feature two small, characterful chimney stacks at each south-facing corner. The right hand side wing, adjoining the orchard, would have housed the private parlours of the Fairfax family, such as Charles Fairfax's study or library. The left wing contained the service quarters, such as a kitchen, buttery and larder etc, and the function of these rooms would have been closely linked with some of the outbuildings to the rear, such as a dairy or brewhouse.

Two datestones survive today on the hall. One is dated 1653, the other 1681, but it is unlikely that they are now in their original positions. There exists at Farnley Hall a stone corner-fireplace with the initials 'CF' and the date 1657 carved on. It is almost certain that this fireplace was once in Charles Fairfax's parlour at Menston, the south room in the right hand wing. It would have been extracted and removed to Farnley, along with the imposing Old Hall gateway, in 1814. From the information gained from these dated artefacts, we can surmise that the exterior of Fairfax's new house might have been completed in 1653, the interior furnishings, panelling etc, finished by 1657, and then further additions and alterations made during the early 1680s, after Charles Fairfax had died.

By the mid-eighteenth century, the Old Hall had fallen into disrepair, possibly because the then absentee Fairfaxes had been 'hard up' for many years and would have been unable to keep their tenanted ancestral home in good repair. When the Old Hall and farm was taken over by the young Walter Hawksworth in 1767 (see on), he immediately proceeded to demolish a considerable part of the house. A tenancy agreement with the Jennings family, dated the 1st September 1767, informs us that Hawksworth 'reserved the Liberty to pull Down Two Wings in the Hall or any other Useless Buildings and Carry them away at will and pleasure'. As a result of the demolition work, Fairfax Old Hall as we see it today is about half its original size. A conjectural impression of the early eighteenth century appearance of the Old Hall, based on surviving old plans and sketches, appears in this book.

Returning to the fortunes of the Fairfaxes, Mary Breary, Charles Fairfax's wife, died in October 1657 (in the same year that the Old Hall interior furnishings appeared to have been completed), having produced nine sons and four daughters. Of this large family, two brothers, John and Henry, were identical twins born in 1634. Their physical features were so alike that not even their mother could tell one brother from another. John was an army captain, his twin brother a clergyman. It was a constant source of amusement and embarrassment to family and friends when Henry the clergyman, who eventually became Dean of Norwich, was mistakenly asked to recall his military exploits, and John the military man was praised for his mild and devout nature! John's only surviving child, Anne Fairfax, married Thomas Pulleyn, a member of a leading Burley-in-Wharfedale family.

Charles Fairfax, antiquarian and genealogist, widower of Mary and father of the thirteen children, died in December 1673, leaving Menston Old Hall in the hands of his eldest son Thomas (1628–1716) and daughter-in-law Dorothy Carliel. This second generation of Menston Fairfaxes remained in residence until around the year 1712, when the now elderly couple retired to Leeds, leaving the Old Hall in the hands of a new tenant, John Pollard. Also in 1712, Thomas and Dorothy Fairfax, with their son the Reverend Thomas Fairfax (born 1673), had to mortgage the Menston family home to Bridget Thornton of Leeds for the sum of £636. (It would appear that the Fairfaxes were short of money at this date and remained so throughout the first half of the century.

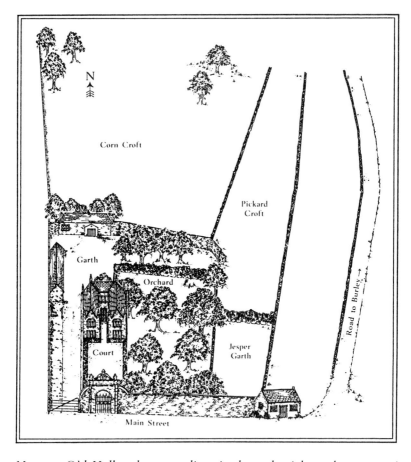

Menston Old Hall and surroundings in the early eighteenth century. A reconstruction by Phillipa Swanton based on surviving early maps and sketches.

The family's chronic financial problems ultimately led to a foreclosure on the mortgage and a forced sale in 1763).

By the year 1717, Thomas Fairfax senior had died and his only son, the Reverend Thomas, now living at Eynsbury in County Huntingdon, was the absentee landlord of the Old Hall. The Fairfaxes were never to return to Menston to live. In 1732 the

Reverend Thomas was made a canon of Lincoln. He died in the year 1744, leaving only one surviving child, a daughter, Elizabeth Fairfax, married to David Middleton of Clifford Street, Westminster, London. Elizabeth and David Middleton sold the Old Hall by a deed of lease and release (the 23rd/24th January 1763) to the brothers Francis and Ayscough Fawkes of Farnley, who were in fact acting on behalf of the young Walter Hawksworth of Hawksworth, then a seventeen year old minor. At this date the Middleton's tenants at Menston were named as William Bailey (at the Old Hall), John Fawcett, John Jennings, Anne Briggs, William Barrett and John Rhodes, the total area of the scattered Old Hall lands being just over 112 acres. When the young Walter Hawksworth came of age in 1767, the Old Hall was handed over to him by the Fawkes and, as we have previously noted, Walter immediately proceeded to arrange the demolition of half the ancestral home of the Fairfaxes.

From 1767 began the long association of the Jennings family and their successors the Popplewells with the Old Hall, an association of family continuity lasting for over 140 years until around 1908. The earliest-known local Jennings can be traced back to Hawksworth, where in 1672 lived William, Edmund and Thomas. Forty years later, a rental for Menston dating from about 1722 shows that some members of the family had moved into the village, farming lands on the eastern side of the township.

On the 1st September 1767, Walter Hawksworth leased to Edmund Jennings the younger, for a period of twenty-one years, 'all that Capitall Messuage Situate at Menston called Mr Fairfax Hall with the Barns and other buildings to the same belonging'. Edmund Jennings was to remain as tenant until his death. He died in the autumn of 1813 in his seventy-fifth year. According to his will, he left to his wife Esther all monies owing to him, the low parlour in the house, the fire irons, a part of a passage with the ground from the parlour nook to the gate, a third part of the front garden and a large prayer book! Edmund also particularly requested that his executor – his son Christopher Jennings – should ensure that his widowed mother Esther be given 'every morning two pints of new milk and sometimes more for nothing and also lead her coals of a good quality for nothing, she paying for the same at the pit'.

Christopher Jennings, representing the next generation of the family at the Old Hall, succeeded his father from 1813 until 1832. Then he relinquished the tenancy in favour of his nephew, young

Edmund Jennings, a direct grandson of the earlier Edmund who died in 1813. However, young Edmund's period of occupation was to last for no more than thirteen years, for in the year 1845 the uncle Christopher Jennings took over again and Edmund and his family left Menston, moving to a destination presently unknown. When the elderly Christopher Jennings died in 1851, his widow Ann decided to remain at the Hall. The couple had had no children. They bequeathed all their interest in the farm, with the crops, cattle, farming implements and all household furniture to a young girl, Sarah Jennings Preston, a great-niece of Mrs Ann Jennings.

Sarah Preston at the age of eighteen married David Popplewell, a local farmer seventeen years her senior. Sadly, Sarah died in 1856 aged only twenty-four, leaving a small child, three year old Christopher Jennings Popplewell. There survives a lease of the Old Hall farm dated the 10th January 1860, made between the landlord, F. H. Fawkes of Farnley on the one part, and the unusual combination of widow Ann Jennings and David Popplewell as joint tenants, on the other part. The family continuity at the Old Hall was maintained during the second half of the century by this David Popplewell, on whose death in 1887 the tenancy was taken over by his son Christopher Jennings Popplewell, now aged about thirty-six. Christopher (known locally as Jennings Popplewell) married Martha Alice Marshall of Mount Stead, Burley, the daughter and heiress of William Marshall who had owned Hill Top Farm, Menston.

The Farnley Fawkes retained their old Fairfax property in Menston until 1896. In that year, the Old Hall and immediate surrounding gardens and outbuildings were sold to a certain Joshua Hart (whose father, the Reverend Joshua Hart, vicar of Otley, had been an enthusiastic local historian.) The outlying fields formerly attached to the hall were sold separately, to become building plots for new housing development. On the 10th July 1896 the new landlord, Joshua Hart, leased to the sitting tenant, Jennings Popplewell, 'the back part of Menston Old Hall, the farm buildings and the right-hand-side garden (from the house to the village)' for £35 per annum. About twelve years later, around 1908, the Popplewells retired and left the hall, so finally ending a very lengthy span of family continuity at Mr Fairfax's old house stretching back to 1767. Jennings Popplewell's grand-daughter, Mrs Vera Horner of Menston, has kindly allowed the writer to browse through her interesting collection of family papers, including a succession of farm leases. The information gleaned

Jennings Popplewell and his wife Martha Alice (née Marshall) of Menston Old Hall.

from this source has been the key to piecing together the family's history.

St John's Parish Church

The history of the church at Menston has been well covered in a booklet produced by members of the parish church, published around 1970 and mainly written by Jean M Heckingbottom, wife of the vicar. The booklet gives quite a few interesting biographical details of the twelve or so vicars who have served Menston parish since the church was consecrated in 1871. One of the most notable of these clergymen was the Reverend Charles Ingham Black (1821–96), an Irishman. It was Mr Black who, shortly after his appointment as incumbent of Burley-in-Wharfedale in 1855, worked energetically to establish an independent parish of Burley with Menston; and, within a year of his arrival, the long-established but by then inconvenient ties with the ancient church at Otley were relinquished.

Not only did Mr Black establish a new parish. He also founded a small chapel of ease for Menston village, a licence for which was granted on the 30th July 1858. The chapel was housed in one of the row of cottages (third from the top) in Derry Hill and was dedicated to St John the Divine. At one time a carved stone cross was to be seen above the doorway into the cottage, but this has disappeared within fairly recent times.

Ten years after the founding of Menston's chapel of ease, Charles Black embarked upon the ambitious scheme of providing the village with its own parish church. Surprisingly, the eventual building and establishment of the new church was done *before* the sale of the Fawkes' Menston farms and the rapid development of Menston new town railway suburb. Although the site for the new edifice was the gift of Bertie Markland, owner of Menston Grange, much of the cost of the so-called 'Anglican revival' at Menston had been subsidised personally by Black and his wife from their own private incomes. For instance, during the first year of the life of the cottage chapel (1858) the Reverend Black provided over fifty per cent of the income of his own church!

The architects of the new parish church were Price and Linklater of Manchester, the chosen style being described by them as 'early Gothic'. The master stonemason on the site was Mr Lapish of Hawksworth, a member of a family established locally in the building trade for many generations; and the joinery work was done by Longley Brothers of Leeds. The stone-laying ceremony took place on the 30th July 1870, the stone being laid by Mrs Hudson of Moorville, whose husband R J Hudson had been a generous benefactor to the cause. The newly-finished edifice was consecrated on the 28th April 1871, the dedication to St John the Divine being transferred from the cottage chapel in Derry Hill.

Moor Croft, Exleys and Menston Methodists

When the former Hitch lands in the village were sold in 1797, there were two purchasers. Griffith Wright bought the grange (see the section on Menston Grange) and Thomas Exley, assisted by Samuel Exley, innkeeper of Apperley Bridge and probably his brother, purchased the remainder of the Hitch's estate, which included a farmstead known as Moor Croft, situated in Main Street. Thomas Exley's son Robert (1787–1867) was later to make his home at Moor Croft with his wife Jane (1791–1851).

The Exley family became leading members of Menston village

society from 1797 until the death of the last-surviving family member, Miss Ellen Exley, in 1924. The home of the Exleys for most of the eighteenth century had been High Rhodes, where they lived as tenants of the Rhodes family of Knaresborough, and where the earliest recorded occupation of the family was that of 'cloth makers'. Succeeding generations of the family were usually described as farmers or yeomen. Two eighteenth century Exley gravestones are to be found in Otley churchyard.

The vicinity of the original Moor Croft homestead (now demolished) is occupied today by the imposing Victorian villa called Croft House, the row of modern brick-built shops called Croft Park and the two Methodist chapels – the original (1826, now an artist's studio) and the larger, later and present one (1886).

It is possible that the name Moor Croft comes from Rector Robert More of Guiseley and his son Timothy, the latter being resident in Menston until his death in 1644. As the Hitches were the successors to the Mores, it is logical that a Hitch farm in the village might have been called Moor Croft after Timothy More, rather than to have been so described because of any connection with moorland. Some of the fields attached to Moor Croft farm – Whiteland Close, Willowland and Stone Stile Close – had been subject to an annual rent charge of £7 in 1797, payable to the schoolmaster of Guiseley to support the church school there. This particular rent charge was established by the will of Robert More, made in 1642, which makes it all the more likely that Moor Croft was called after a family of that name.

Methodism flourished at Menston from the mid-eighteenth century, at a time when all the local towns and villages formed part of the great 'Haworth Round' of travelling preachers. Yeadon had the earliest recorded local meetings, dating from 1742. Two years later Methodists in Menston and Bingley joined the circuit. The Exley family of High Rhodes and Moor Croft were very active in promoting the early Methodist cause by donating land in Moor Croft for a site for the first chapel, by becoming leading benefactors of the chapel, and by helping to establish a Methodist day school on the south side of Main Street, the original building of which (1830) now survives as a joiner's and undertaker's work-shop.

The founding deed for the original chapel, dated the 24th March 1826, was made between Robert Exley, yeoman (the donor of the site) and the following Menston residents: Christopher Jennings, Jeremiah Watmough, John Rhodes and John Jennings (farmers); John Muschamp (stone mason); Henry Hanson (tailor); Jeremiah

Wood and John Shepherd (woolcombers); and of Otley, George Sheppard, gentleman.

The deed describes a plot of land comprising 140 square yards which had been staked off from a larger close called Moor Croft, bounded on the south by the town street of Menston. The trustees were granted full liberty to 'make put out opcn and at all times hereafter to have and enjoy as many windows or lights in the east, west and north walls or sides of the chapel or meeting house when the same shall be erected'. The building eventually constructed (possibly by John Muschamp the stonemason) still exists in Menston today: it is the plain, functional and box-like edifice which stands near the road junction, to the west of the present Methodist chapel (1886).

One story which has been handed down through a few generations of Menstonians is the one about the dispute between the local Methodist trustees and Ayscough Fawkes of Farnley. The dispute, which arose in 1871, concerned the true ownership of the Methodist day school, which apparently had been built on a part of the common which was once Farnley Estate land, and for which Ayscough Fawkes was demanding a ground rent of some kind or other and which the Methodists were refusing to pay. A meeting took place in the schoolroom. At one side of the table sat one of the Exleys of the day: opposite him sat Mr Fawkes; and between them, lying on the table, was the key to the schoolroom. Somehow or other, it was agreed that whichever of the two parties could remain at the table for the longest period of time would be the 'winner' of the dispute! The two men sat opposite each other, arms folded in determined mood, for many an hour. Night fell, the hour grew late and still the two remained in stubborn silence. Then in the cold light of dawn, Ayscough Fawkes wearily rose from the table, left the building and his claims on the property were shortly afterwards dropped.

Kirklands and Fourness House

The site now occupied by the large Victorian Community Centre is of some interest in the annals of Menston's history. We must not forget that the present house name is of fairly recent origin. Before the name Kirklands was coined, the house and an earlier dwelling on the same site were long known as Fourness House. During the late nineteenth century, the building was occupied by members of the leading Exley family.

Before the time of the Exleys, the house and former adjoining smallholding belonged to Miss Mary Rhodes, who had died in about 1872. Miss Rhodes had inherited the property from her father Christopher, a yeoman of Creskeld Hall, Arthington, and her grandfather Joseph Rhodes of Menston. It is very probable that these Rhodes were connected to the earlier families of the same name resident in the village.

Joseph Rhodes had in fact originally purchased the Menston homestead and eleven acres of adjoining farmland (named Ling Croft, New Close, Greenlands, Partlands and Waterholme) from Tobias Fourness, yeoman of Wakefield Outwood, on the 13th January 1769. This explains how the present Kirklands site was originally known as Fourness House.

To go back further in time, we discover that the hearth tax roll of 1672 shows a Thomas 'ffurnice' to be living on this site in a home with four hearths, one of the larger homes in Menston at that date. Thomas had been preceded by Walter Fourness (living in 1630) who in turn was preceded by his own parents, William and Anne.

This Anne Fourness was a younger daughter of John Breary of Menston Old Hall, and so the Walter Fourness of 1630 must have been a cousin of both the Rhodes and the Fairfaxes.

John 'Fornes', a 'bilman parcell harnyd abill person', complete with his horse, is listed in the Menston muster roll of 1539.

We could continue our backwards motion, peeling off further layers of local history, but time and space compels the writer to stop here and leave more detailed researches to others.

Low Hall

When Jeffrey Rhodes of High Rhodes made out his will on the 4th February 1671, he appointed 'my kinsman Richard Rhodes of Menston' as one of the executors. This Richard Rhodes was living in a house on the site of the present Low Hall. He was a kinsman of Jeffrey's in more ways than one for, as well as being a relative on the Rhodes side, there was also an additional link through the Brearys of Menston Old Hall: two Breary sisters Isobel and Margaret had each married a Rhodes towards the end of the sixteenth century, Isobel marrying John Rhodes of the High Rhodes and Margaret marrying John Rhodes of Menston.

Four generations of Low Hall Rhodes can be linked together, commencing with the Richard mentioned in the previous paragraph who was born circa 1625, and finishing with the last

A datestone and door lintel from Low Hall, Menston, now placed in a house at Harden, Bingley. Drawn by Jack Kell.

resident member, John Rhodes, who died in 1751. By the early eighteenth century the Rhodes family of Menston were numbered among the local minor gentry, as the wording on their tombstones, still to be seen in Otley churchyard, indicates.

The earliest known Low Hall, shown to have had four hearths at the time of the 1672 tax roll, was rebuilt by the first Richard Rhodes in 1685. For many years a datestone bearing his initials and this date was to be seen in the gardens of the hall, but the stone has now been removed to a house at Harden, Bingley. Low Hall was rebuilt a second time, apparently in 1744 for the last John Rhodes, this new building – being altogether of a much grander design – still forming the south central section of the present house.

The farmlands attached to the hall lay in a compact group of fields immediately behind the house, and included what is now the cricket pitch behind the Fox and Hounds inn. Further northwards, the farm stretched down to Ellar Ghyll and Acrecliff, and extended across the parish boundary into Otley. Low Hall fields in the mid-eighteenth century were named as: West Croft, Holm Field, Ashold

Ing, Lamb Close, East Croft, Moor Flatts, three closes called Moor Riddings, New Close, Near Kirk Briggs, Farr Kirk Briggs, Partlands, Blake Riddings, West Acre Cliff and Middle Acre Cliff, all in Menston; and in Otley, East Acre Cliff, Storrys, Steward Ridding and Gascoyne Land. These fields were connected to Low Hall by a small gated road; and a short section of this farmtrack still survives – now in the form of the public footway immediately to the north of the cricket pitch.

   The first Richard Rhodes – the one who had rebuilt his home in 1685 – died in 1703 at the age of seventy-seven, leaving two children, John and Anne. John in turn died in 1720 leaving five children, namely: the eldest son Richard (1690–1734), who succeeded at the hall; a second son John, who after matriculating at St John's College Cambridge (1714) became Vicar of Ilkley until his death in 1727; a third son William who moved to Burley-in-Wharfedale and who was father of Jeremiah Rhodes of Otley; a daughter Anne who remained a spinster; and a daughter Beatrix who married Zachariah Collier, a member of a leading Yeadon family.

   After the second Richard Rhodes died in 1734 at the age of forty-four, his offspring were four young children, Elizabeth (then aged about 14), John (12), Anne (7) and Eleanor (4). The only son, John, had great ambitions to rebuild his great-grandfather's house in an imposing and expensive fashion, and as soon as he came of age (1744) he plunged into a grand rebuilding scheme which resulted in the central part of Low Hall as we know it today. In order to raise the necessary capital for the rebuilding project, John had to mortgage the whole of his Menston estate to his brother-in-law John Hird (husband of his older sister Elizabeth), who was a wealthy tallow chandler from Buckstone in Rawdon.

   Unfortunately, young John Rhodes was not to enjoy the impressive splendours of his new imposing mansion for very long: he became ill, and within eight years had died, apparently a bachelor. He was the last Rhodes of Low Hall. His property had to be sold to repay the mortgage. A contemporary memorandum at the time states that John's estate included 'the mansion house wherein he lately lived etc almost new and in good repair, seven cattle gates on Menston Common, a wood, and Bishop lands in the township of Otley. Upon the sale of the premises there must be reserved a road (for the convenience of the premises lying at Storris and the lands thereto adjoining) through the Fold where Mr Rhodes lately lived and so down the lane leading to Acrecliff for carriage, cattle'.

Low Hall; the south front, circa 1744.

Included in the details of John Rhodes' will, made on the 15th October 1751, was reference to the sum of £20 to be invested after his death by trustees, the interest arising from the capital to be paid on St John's Day each year among the poor of Menston. This was the origin of the so-called Rhodes Charity, in existence for many years following. (Appendix 5 shows the personal inventory of John Rhodes, made on the 30th November 1751.)

In 1753, Low Hall was sold to Walter Hawksworth, and remained part of the Hawksworth and Fawkes estate in Menston until 1876. On the 25th April 1753, Walter Hawksworth leased to John Marshall 'all that capital messuage in Menston wherein the late Mr John Rhodes deceased formerly dwelt'. The wording of the lease contains a curious clause which states that Walter Hawksworth reserved for his own use 'two rooms in the said messuage called the hall or hall body and the dining room and also two chambers and a closet over the same rooms; the three stalled stable, the orchard and the garden'. Marshall was not allowed to occupy these parts of the premises. In addition, the tenant was obliged to 'make and keep fires in the rooms above mentioned at all times', the cost of the coals being paid for by Walter Hawksworth.

Why the new purchaser should wish to reserve these rooms for himself remains a complete mystery. The implication in the wording of the lease is that the rooms specified should be constantly aired and ready for occupation at all times and without notice. Walter Hawksworth had been a close friend and contemporary of John Rhodes. Perhaps he wished to keep alive the memory of his friend by preserving intact some of the rooms at Low Hall exactly as John Rhodes had left them.

For the next 120 years Low Hall remained a tenanted farm. Then, on the 28th September 1876, the hall, with some of the immediately surrounding lands of around fifteen acres, was sold to James Padgett, a wealthy cloth manufacturer. The Padgetts were as keen to make alterations to the hall as John Rhodes had been in his day: they added a new wing to the east side of the 1744 house, and on the west side grafted on an imposing new entrance, forming part of an ostentatious and fanciful square tower. (In 1936 the tower had to be demolished as a result of fire damage.) The Padgetts remained at Low Hall until around 1914. During their stay, they constructed the long and imposing row of stone terrace houses known as Marlborough Villas on one of the hall fields. This terrace, with its tower house at the Bradford Road end, was seen by some locals as reminiscent of a steam train; and the derisory nickname 'Puffing Billy Terrace' was given to the row which was built, it is believed, for some of the Padgett senior workpeople employed in the family mill.

On the 16th March 1914, the hall, Marlborough Villas and various lots of nearby building land were sold by auction at the Hare and Hounds Hotel by Oliver, Appleton and Kitchen. The new owners of Low Hall were the Butterfields, a family with prosperous business connections at Shipley. They were to continue to live at the old house of the Rhodes, with its Padgett extensions, until around 1964. Then Mr Clifford Butterfield, the representative of the family at that date, made a magnanimous gesture: he gave to the people of Menston, as a parting gift, the large private field to the south of the house, this gesture enabling today's much valued public recreation park to be created. The hall itself, with new extensions and internal alterations, became an elderly persons' home.

The Inns and Taverns of Menston

Of the four public houses within Menston, the oldest established would appear to be the Fox and Hounds, the earliest record of which dates from 1822 when the landlord was Samuel Jennings. However, the inn was not on its present site; it was in fact located in the centre of the old village, at Lane Ends. According to a certain Albert Hancock who died in the 1930s at the age of seventy, his father had told him that the original 'Fox' existed where the steps up to St John's Parish Church are now.

The removal of the sign to its present location on the main road, a strategically good move from the point of view of passing trade, took place in 1849. On the 1st December that year, Francis Hawksworth Fawkes leased to John Jennings of Menston, farmer, a newly-built house, erected at Jenning's own expense, 'used as an inn and known by the name or sign of Fox and Hounds'. It is highly likely that John Jennings was a close relative of the Samuel who was landlord of the old Fox in 1822, and also a cousin of those Jennings who were farming at Hill Top and Fairfax Old Hall.

John Jennings died in 1851 aged eighty-four, to be succeeded by his grandson, also named John Jennings, who farmed about forty acres behind the inn. By 1861, John and his wife Grace were living at the Fox with four young children – Grace, Mary, John and Margaret; but the family had disappeared from Menston altogether by 1871, the licensee at the inn now being George Craven and his wife Sarah.

The Hare and Hounds has been in existence since the early 1840s and is believed to be Menston's second oldest licensed premises, although the present building (dating from the 1930s) obviously replaces a much older one on or near the same spot. The Hare had associations in former years with the Watkinson and Hustler families. Samuel Watkinson was in residence as landlord by 1841. He was still there ten years later, a widower, living with two unmarried daughters Sarah and Mary and two sons Jonathan and Richard, who were both kept busy as woolcombers in the well-established local worsted industry. By the 1860s, the Watkinsons had been replaced by Jonas Hustler, a Shipley man, who, like his neighbours the Jennings of the Fox, had a smallholding of about forty acres attached to the inn. During the 1880s, Hustler was succeeded by James and Mary Walls.

The attractive range of house and former attached farm building at Menston Lane Ends, now occupied by the Malt Shovel public house, has a history dating back to at least the middle of the last century. The public house is believed to have taken its name from associations with a former maltkiln, which was being used by John Riley in the 1820s. Whether the maltkiln was situated at the present inn, or whether it was nearby at the now-demolished Maltkiln Row, standing on the site of the former church hall, we do not know. The property on both sides of the road belonged to Griffith Wright, owner of Menston Grange.

In 1850, the innkeeper of the Shovel was Timothy Fawcett, a young married man with a three year old daughter, Hannah. Ten years later the publicans were another young couple, William and Jane Popplewell, who had come from Hawksworth. The Spencer family were in residence during the 1870s, followed by Isabella Wilson, a widow, and her niece Mary Thompson in the early 1880s.

The youngest of Menston's inns is the Menston Arms. This is believed to have begun its life as a simple, down-to-earth beer shop, forming part of Bradley's Buildings, existing in the 1870s and established by Richard Bradley, an agricultural labourer. The present premises appear to be of late nineteenth century date, and the arms displayed on the inn sign (a black rampant lion) are those of the Fairfax family of nearby Menston Old Hall.

List of Appendices

Appendix 1: Grant of a licence from the Archbishop of York for a chapel at Hawksworth, 1343; followed by an inventory and rental of the dower of Jane Hawksworth, widow, 1549.

Appendix 2: The Fightin' 'Auxworths, 1547 and 1678–80.

Appendix 3: Notes about the boundaries of Hawksworth, from various sources, 1273, 1733 and 1901.

Appendix 4: Some local residents, 1379, 1539 and 1672.

Appendix 5: Inventory of the goods and chattels of Mr John Rhodes of Menston (Low Hall), 1751.

Appendix 6: The building of High Royds Hospital – as reported in the columns of the *Wharfedale and Airedale Observer*, 1886–8.

Appendix 7: A report and valuation of the Hawksworth Estate for F H Fawkes by Hollis and Webb, May 1900.

Appendix 8: Hawksworth auction sale, 1919, from the pages of the *Yorkshire Evening Post*.

Appendix 1:

The Archbishop's Licence concerning the Chapel at Hawksworth, 1343.

William, by divine permission Archbishop of York,[1] Primate of England, Ambassador of the Apostolic See, gives greeting, grace and blessing to his beloved son Walter of Hawksworth:
We, favourably inclined to your pious requests that you should be permitted to have divine service lawfully celebrated by a suitable chaplain in the excellent chapel situated within your manor of Hawksworth in our diocese, as long as by this action there is in no way creation of any prejudice to the parish church of that place, grant to you and that same chaplain by these present letters full power to do this at our continuing great pleasure. Farewell, dated at Bradford, 11th October A.D. 1343 and the second year of our archiepiscopy.
Translated from the original Latin by Oliver Pickering and Wendy Childs. Source:The Gaunt Papers.

[1]The Archbishop in question is William Zouche, elected 1340 and consecrated 1342.

Inventory and Rental of the Dower of Jane daughter of Alexander Paslewe, widow of Walter Hawksworth, 1549.

Hawksworth Hall: The Chappell, the Parlour, the chappell chamber, the new chamber, the gatehouse chamber and ye calf house.
One close Crabtree flat with Raw Rode 13/4
Miln Hill with Lund Spring 10/-
One close called conygarth with parcell of sunnybanke spring 10/-
One close called Cop rode with parcell of sunnybanke Spring 23/4
One close Sunny rode feild with Eves spring 23/4
One close called the Lund 13/4
Source: The Gaunt Papers.

Appendix 2:

The Fightin' 'Auxworths, 1547 and 1678–80

1547
'Walter Hawksworth - - - being slaine at the battle of Musselbrough (1547), where having past two charges, through a body of the Scotts, in ye third charge, his horse being killed and hee himselfe beeing fastened in his saddle (after the manner of those times) he was there slaine.'
(Source: a mid-seventeenth century bound volume of Hawksworth family memoranda, now part of the Gaunt Papers.)

1678
'Sr Walter Hawksworth's lady being with child and affrighted with her husbands causing his men to shoot off pistols close to the house, travelled and brought forth two children. December 1678.'

1680
'Upon Lord's Day, May 30th 1680, at Hawksworth, there were several gentlemen drinking and ranting at a strange rate, amongst whom was one Hawksworth, uncle to Sr Walter Hawksworth, who lives there, and one Sherburn, who was more outragious than the rest, and grievously provokt this Hawksworth, challenging him to a fight. Sr Walter fetcht his uncle a rapier, and sd. 'If you be an Hawksworth, try it with him'. They both went out, Sherburn let fly at him, Hawksworth defended himself, would have ceased, but the other was so desperate raging that he turned again, run him into the brest, Sherburn was carryed in dyed presently, oh dredful!

'Last Easter at that very place at Hawksworth on a Lords day 2 men were playing at ball, the one hit the other on the brest, and he fell down dead, yet they sin still.'
Source: extracts from the Diary of Oliver Heywood, a Yorkshire Puritan minister, 1678 and 1680.

Appendix 3:

Notes about the boundaries of Hawksworth, from various sources, 1273, 1733 and 1901

Gift of land in Hawksworth from Simon Ward to Walter Hawksworth, 1273

Know, present and future, that I, Simon, son of Simon Ward, have given, granted, and with my present charter confirmed to Walter, son of Walter of Hawksworth, and the legitimate heirs of his body, all my land and rents in the vill of Hawksworth, with the demesne land or the demesne lands of the same vill, and with all rights of common and easements, also in the moors, marshes, woods, turbaries, meadows, fields and pastures, and with all the appurtenances belonging to the aforesaid vill without any retention, as they are contained within the boundaries of the said demesne between the lordship of Bingley on the south and the lordship of Burley on the north: that is to say beginning at Old Wood Beck, and so climbing Knapley Hill, and so to Cocklay Hill, and Altonthorne, and so to Hornclif Well, and so to Romslaw, and descending by the way called the way to York as far as the Grey Mere, and so following the Sike as far as Hollgill, and Chapel Croft, and so following the Black Sike as far as White Cross; to hold and to have all the aforesaid tenements with their appurtenances to the aforesaid Walter and the legitimate heirs of his body, freely and quietly of me and my heirs for ever. And if the aforesaid Walter or his heirs should die without legitimate heirs of their body, the aforesaid tenements with their appurtenances shall revert fully to me (Simon) and my heirs. And truly I, Simon, and my heirs, guarantee and make quit for ever to the aforesaid Walter and the legitimate heirs of his body all the aforesaid tenements with their appurtenances against all men. In witness of which thing I place my seal to this present charter, with these witnesses: Sir William de Stopham senior, Sir Richard Wallace, Sir Robert Plumpton, knights, John of Stapelton, Richard Babington, Walter of Midelton, Lawrence of Arthington, and many others. 1 Edward 1, A.D. 1273. *Translation from the original Latin by Oliver Pickering and Wendy Childs.* *Source: the Gaunt Papers.*

1733: Legal evidences about boundaries

Richard Barret of Hawksworth Aged 70 years and being no Tenant of Sr Walter Hawksworth Saith That he very well Remembers the Boundarys of Hawksworth what makes him remember more perticularly He was the Moor grave Three and twenty years and No Disturbance during that time about the Boundarys And during that time they never graved Turfes on the South Side York Way to his knowledge which he always tooke to be the Boundary Betwixt Burleigh and Hawksworth And very well remembers Rums Law which lyes a Considerable Distance North West of Skirtfull of Stones, Which Rums Law is a Round Ring of Stones which at present has a Stoop Sett in the Middle of it And also remembers Skirtfull of Stones which he never heard go by any other Name than Skirtfull of Stones And that the Old York Way went by Rums Law on the North Side of Skirtfull of Stones which he will Swear to.

Thomas Ambler of Hawksworth Aged near Eighty years Deposeth and Saith that he has no Interest in the Common of Hawksworth being and receiving the Poor Sess from the Town of Hawksworth But further Saith that he has Road Sr Walter Hawksworths Boundaries and has always been Directed by very Ancient Men Which was the Old Boundaries And further Saith That he very well Remembers the Boundaries And that the Boundaries were from Horncliff Well Directly in a line to Rums Law from thence to a New Sett Stoope On York Way or by York Way And that the said Thomas Ambler was at the Setting of the present Stoops of the Boundaries which goes from Horncliffe Well to Rums Law and those was the Old Boundaries near 50 years agoe, And from Rums Law to a Stoop lately Sett up nigh York way And then to North Side of Skirtfull of Stones which said Skirtfull of Stones was never a Boundary nor never went by any other Name than Skirtfull of Stones as he remembers. And then to two Boundaries of Mr Pulleynes And then to Bee Stone as Called all his time; and all these Boundaries in a Direct Line to Bee Stone being the Old Boundary; And remembers a Stoop being Sett up with this Inscription T:P: This is Rums Law which sd Stoop is removed but cant tell where nor by whom it was set up quite to another part of the Comon And this Thomas Ambler will Depose upon Oath.

Legal evidence produced in a boundary dispute between Sir Walter Hawksworth of Hawksworth and Thomas Pulleyne of Burley-in-Wharfedale. Source: Farnley Hall Papers.

1901: Boundary Markers

'Mr Turner led the way across Burley Moor to the Great Skirtful of Stones, a huge cairn of small boulders, nearly a hundred tons on a heap, although for centuries loads have been taken away to mend the trackways across the moor. The ancient British trackway and the Roman road were also indicated. The centre of the cairn is now hollow, as it was explored many years ago, and from the middle human bones were taken, and submitted to Canon Greenwell and other archaeologists. The cairn lies eastwards from the shooting house, or Grubstone box, a conspicuous object from all the highlands around Bradford. To us in these parts it seems like a round tower, but near at hand it is found to be a square tower, and the windows of the two stories, as also the floor and roof are wanting. A smaller cairn of great interest lies nearer the shooting box, in the centre of which is a boundary stone of 150 years ago or more, bearing the name of Mr Hawksworth, and the words,

'THIS IS RUMBLES LAW'

Mr Turner explained that 'law' was always used in the British sense for a hill, and Rumbles Hill, or cairn, was a conspicuous boundary mark for many centuries. He had found in the Burley Manor Rolls, two centuries back, that on Rogation Day, when the boundaries were beaten by the inhabitants, they met on this hill, and describing their boundaries, they concluded the nominy by joining in the words, 'This is Rumbles Law'.

From the pages of the Shipley Express, *1901.*

Appendix 4:

Some local residents, 1379, 1539, and 1672

Poll Tax Roll, 2 Richard II (1379)

Hewkesworth

Symon Warde, Chiualer, & vx	xx.s.
Adam Walkar & vx	iiij.d.
Walterus Thomson & vx	iiij.d.
Johannes Hyne & vx	iiij.d.
Henricus Turnour & vx	iiij.d.
Thomas Schephird & vx	iiij.d.
Johannes Wynne & vx	iiij.d.
Thomas Byschop & vx	iiij.d.
Ricardus Schephird & vx	iiij.d.

Johannes Knayp & vx   iiij.d.
Ricardus filius Willelmi & vx   iiij.d.
Johannes de Bynglay & vx   iiij.d.
Johannes de Roudon & vx   iiij.d.
Johannes Watson & vx   iiij.d.
Willelmus Smyth & vx   iiij.d.
Henricus ffouler & vx   iiij.d.
Adinet del fforest & vx   iiij.d.
Ricardus Waltheu & vx   iiij.d.
Alicia relicta Johannis   iiij.d.
Beatrix relicta Radulfi   iiij.d.
Willelmus seruiens Willelmi   iiij.d.
Henricus filius Adynet   iiij.d.
Johanna filia Ricardi   iiij.d.
Alicia filia Ricardi   iiij.d.
Alicia filia Willelmi   iiij.d.
Johannes de Haworth   iiij.d.
Matilda Rendurer   iiij.d.
Agnes de Bradelay   iiij.d.
Willelmus ffouler   iiij.d.

           Summa xxix.s. iiij.d.

Menston

Johannes del Rodes & vx   iiij.d.
Johannes Picard & vx   iiij.d.
Willelmus filius Thome & vx   iiij.d.
Walterus Grauer & xv   iiij.d.
Willelmus filus Ricardi & vx   iiij.d.
Hugo de Gomersall & vx   iiij.d.
Willelmus Picard & vx   iiij.d.
Ricardus Picard & vx   iiij.d.
Hugo Picard & vx   iiij.d.
Thomas Brer & vx   iiij.d.
Willelmus de Brerhagh & vx   iiij.d.
Johannes filus Thome & vx   iiij.d.
Johannes Merebek & vx   iiij.d.
Agnes del Rodes   iiij.d.
Emma Picard   iiij.d.
Johannes Wateman   iiij.d.
Johannes Picard   iiij.d.
Willelmus Brer   iiij.d.
Johannes Brer   iiij.d.
Stephanus del Walles   iiij.d.
Alicia relicta Willelmi   iiij.d.

Henricus Merebek   iiij.d.
Johannes Elynson   iiij.d.

Summa vij.s. viij.d.

The Musters in Skyrack Wapentake, 1539

The Township of Hawkysworthe

Thes be bilmen, abill persons, parcell harnessed:
  Thomas Hertley; jake, par splent (pair of splints).
  Thomas Wood: horse, jake.
  Thomas Ball: jake and salett.
  William Snyddon (?); a sallett.
  John Hertley; jake and sallyt.
  Christofer Stell; jake and sallett.
Thes be archers having no harnes, fotmen, abill persons:
  Christofer Pekard (?)
  Richerd Clapham.
  John Wylson.
  Robert Sadler.
  Jamez Mytton.
  Nicholas Rodes.
  Bryan Beston; jake.
  Robert Barton; jake.
  William Hertley.
Thes be bilmen hauyng no harnes, fotmen, abill persons:
  Thomas Obson,
  Robert Knolles,
  John Rodes,
  William Craven,
  Thomas Jennyng,
  Roger Dykson,
  William Kyrkbe,
  Thomas Walkar,
  John Pollerd.

The Township of Menston

Archers horsed and harnessed, abill persons:
  Christofer Pekard,
  John Pekard,
  William Lyster,
  William Huddylston.
Archers parcell harnessed, abill persons:
  William Roydes; a horse.
  Thomas Hawksworthe.
  Antony Hawksworthe.

Thez be bilmen parcell harnyd, abill persons:
William Mathewe; a horse.
John Fornes; a horse.
Nicholas Cromok; a horse.
Thomas Lyster; a horse.
Robert Bank; a horse.
Christofer Mytton; a horse.
Item: horse and harnes for a man in comon in the Town.

Hearth Tax Roll, 1672
(The number given after each name refers to the number of hearths)

Hawkesworth

Walter Hawkeworth Esq	17	Joseph Blades	2
Walter Calverley Esq	14	John Milner	1
Nath. Collier	3	John Garnett	1
Willm Marshall	3	ffr. Cowling	1
Josias Collier	2	Tho. Batt	1
Samuell Marshall	1	John Padgett	2
Joseph Marshall	1	John Hartley, jun.	3
John Halliday	1	Widd. Cliffe	2
Timothy Overend	1	John Rhoades	2
Widdow Daniell	1	John Hartley, sen.	3
Will. Bartle	1	Will Parrish	1
Widdow Bake	1	Tho. Pawson	1
Will. Bolton	1	Willm Long	1
Tho. Ward	1	Ephraim Marshall	1
Geo. Nelson	2	Samuell Longbotham	1
Tho. Pollard	1	John Harrison	1
Ri. Rhoades	2		
Will. Hawksworth	1		98
Jo. Nicholls, sen.	1		—
John Nicholls, jun.	2		
Wid' Pulland	1		
ffran. Pulland	1	These psons ffollowing	
Will. Roades	1	are discharged by	
Edm. Watson	1	certificate:–	
Widd' Mitton	2	Wid. Tomson	1
Chr. Mitton	2	Widd. Turner	1
Wid. Jenings	1	Rich. Wood	1
John Eastburne	1	Omitted by reason of	
Willm Jenings	1	poverty	1
Edm. Jenings	1		
Tho. Jenings	1		
Wid' Holmes	2		
Tho. Ambler	2		

Menston

Charles ffairfax Esq	13	Ri. Sowden	1
Mr Richard Rhoads	4	Geo. Pollard	1
Mr John Fairfax	5	Robte Walker	2
Lawrence Curtasse	1	Rich. Walker	1
Willm Curtasse	1	William Roades	1
John Pickard	1	Rich. Ryley	1
Robt Oldfeild	1	Widd. Wilson	1
Chro. Pickard	1	John Rhoades	1
Jerom Overend	1	John Walker	1
John Wells	1	Willm Tidewell	1
Widd. Nelson	1	John Watson	1
Miles ffranckland	1	Willm Ryley	1
Mr Mawde	2	John Tompson	1
Charles Watson	1	Tho. Surr	1
Geo. Roades	1		—
Laur. Curtice	1		57
Widd. Marshall	1		—
Peter Spetch	1	Omitted by reason of	
Thomas ffurnice	4	poverty	2

Source: various publications of the Yorkshire Archaeological Society and the Thoresby Society)

Appendix 5:

An Appraisment of all the Goods & Chattels belonging to the late Mr John Rhodes of Menston (Low Hall) deceased taken 30th of November 1751 —

purse & apparel	20	0	0
plate	7	10	0
Linnen	2	5	0
Goods in the Hall two tables		16	0
A Range		5	6
Seven Chairs	1	10	0
A Old Spinnett		15	0
fifteen pictures		10	0
Dining Room Two Tables		18	0
Six Chairs	1	4	0
A Range		10	0
Stair Case An Eight Days Clock	4	0	0
Thirty Small pictures		10	0
Little parlour Bed and Bedding	1	12	0
A small Table		2	6
four pictures		1	6
A Range		2	0

In the Kitchin A Range etc		12	0
Jack and Grate	1	4	0
Fender Tongs & poker		7	0
Two sets Tongs & fenders		16	0
dresser & pewter case	1	4	0
48 of pewter at 8d ea.	1	12	0
Two tables & one Stand		6	6
a Longsettle		5	0
Six Chairs		3	6
a Tea Kettle & Coffee Can		6	0
a Warming pan and Brass Mortar		5	0
a Copper Can & a Copper dish		4	0
a Copper posnett & cover		3	6
a Pain Oven & dripping pan		3	0
a sett pot & Grate etc		4	6
a Screen		6	0
a pair of Bellows		1	6
a Smoothing Iron		2	6
a Small Seeing Glass			6
a Small Cupboard		1	0
a Tin Dish Cover			6
Curtain Rod & Curtain		2	0
a Cross Bow		2	6
4 delfe dishes & 6 plates		2	6
a Tea Chest & China Ware		8	0
Glass Ware		5	0
In the scullery a set pan etc		3	6
a Flaskitt & Warter Kitt		2	0
In the Back Kitchin A Brewing pan & grate	1	10	0
a Backstone & a Range		7	0
An old Table & huslement		4	0
In the Cellar Brewing Vessels		8	0
10 barrells at 2s a piece	1	0	0
3 dozen of bottles		6	0
2 Gantrys		2	0
In the pantry A Churn etc		2	6
Bowls and Trenchers		3	0
A Kemlin		2	6
potts and huslement stuffe		2	6
In the Hall Chamber, A Range & End Irons		4	0
Two Tables		10	0
Three Chairs		4	6
A dozen small pictures		4	0
An old Close Stool & pott		3	0
In Another Chamber one Bedstead and Bedding	3	3	0
A Small Table		2	6
6 chairs		12	0

a Range		1	6
a Large Box		3	0
In a Clossett a Writing desk & some Books	1	6	0
A wing glass		6	6
Kitchin Chamber one Bedstead & Bedding	1	10	0
A La-(?) Bedstead & Bedding		18	0
An old Ark		3	6
Six pictures		2	0
In the Garrett an Old Ark		3	0
An Old Bedstead		6	0
In the Clossett a Table		4	0
a Stand		2	0
Three Old Gunns	1	4	0
Knives & Forks		5	0
Husbandry Gear	1	1	0
One Old Mare	2	0	0
A Scotch Galloway	2	10	0
A Young Mare Three Years Old	3	15	0
One Calveing Cow	3	10	0
A Cow & Calfe	4	0	0
80 sheep at 4s a peice	16	0	0
Sow & two piggs		15	0
Three Asses		6	0
Corn in Barns	20	0	0
Hay	5	0	0
a Malt Mill		10	0

Total   £127 15 6

We whose names are underwritt are witnesses to the above praisment –
William Mawde
Nathaniel Kendall
Jonathan Ouldfield
John Jennings.

Source: York Ecclesiastical Archives, Borthwick Institute, York.

Appendix 6:

The building of High Royds Hospital – as reported in the columns of the Wharfedale and Airedale Observer, 1886–8.

Friday March 19th 1886. Letter to the Editor.

West Riding Asylum, Menston.

Sir, In your issue of February 5th last you very kindly permitted and aided me by your kind words to appeal therein on behalf of the distressed workmen of the above buildings, who had then been unemployed for several weeks through the severe weather, which has continued down to the time of writing. The result is the whole of the masons, bricklayers, labourers and navvies have had to endure enforced idleness and consequences for upwards of three months. Their trials and sufferings increasing, to their credit many of them have refrained as long as possible from accepting that, which, through the exceeding great kindness and generosity of the gentry and others of the neighbourhood, we have been enabled to supply them with, viz: soup and bread, of which some 300 now partake of once daily; occasionally giving out, in small quantities according to the needs and number of families, coals, tea and sugar, or a small sum of money. If this state of thing continues we shall have to depend on the help of our richer friends for the continuance of that support which has enabled us for six weeks to do much good, and for which, Sir, we are truly thankful.

It is impossible to trespass upon your space to name the kind donors all round, but with your permission, I take the liberty of saying that to Mr. M. W. Thompson of Park Gate – well, no words of mine can adequately thank him for his unbound generosity – but he, along with Mr Ayscough Fawkes, Mr F. Darwin, Mr W. Fison, Mr Arnold-Forster, Mr and Mrs Thomas Horsfall, Mr James Bastow, Mr Jas. Hodson, Mrs Horsfall (Old Hall), Mr Reginald Thompson, Hollings Hill, and Messrs Duncan Bros., Otley Mills – (but I must stop) may rest assured that among the many will be found those who will ever remember their kindness with deep gratitude. In conclusion I may just say that Mrs Horsfall, and her niece Miss Mullen of Manningham have constantly assisted Mrs Webb in the making and distributing of soup etc. Mrs Horsfall, we regret to say, has been taken ill in consequence, and also Mrs A. Hasse, of Menston, who commenced to help us, but had to desist. The Vicar of Menston has greatly helped the poor of the parish.

Apologising for the length of letter, I will just add that strict accounts of income and expenditure are kept. Any donor so desiring can satisfy themselves on that point by applying at the Lodge; and, with your permission, either myself or someone else may give the total amounts collected and distributed.

Thanking you in anticipating your kindness in publishing this – I am, Sir, your obedient servant,

H. WEBB   Clerk of Works

March 16th 1886

Friday July 16th 1886

A **Cricket match** was played with 44 of the asylum men (masons and bricklayers) near the Malt Shovel Hotel, Menston, on Saturday. Play was continued till seven o'clock, when the game ended in a draw. Eighty persons sat down to a knife-and-fork tea, which was provided at the Malt Shovel, and an enjoyable evening was spent in music, singing, and dancing & etc.

Friday March 9th 1888

Appointment of Medical Superintendent for Menston Asylum

At the last Christmas Quarter Sessions for the West Riding of Yorkshire, Mr Basil T. Woodd alluded to the progress made with the Menston Lunatic Asylum buildings, and said it was hoped by the autumn the interior fittings would be so far advanced that the committee of Justices might be able to make room for patients from the Wakefield and Wadsley Asylums, which at that time were crowded. He added that at the next meeting of the committee steps would be taken to appoint an experienced medical superintendent, who would be able to assist the committee with regard to the furnishing of the buildings and other matters. The committee afterwards advertised for a medical superintendent, the salary offered being £400 per annum, together with board and furnished residence. It was a condition that the candidates should not be less than twenty-eight nor more than forty years of age, that they should be duly qualified medical practicioners, and have had experience in the treatment of lunatics. There were 29 applications, which were reduced to seven. A meeting of the committee was held yesterday, in the West Riding Magistrates' Room at Leeds Town Hall for the purpose of making the appointment. Mr Basil T. Woodd (the chairman of the committee) presided, and there was a large attendance of members. The seven selected candidates appeared before the committee, and after consideration, Dr J. G. McDowall, Senior Assistant Medical Officer at the Wadsley Asylum, was elected. Dr McDowall, who is thirty-six years of age, is a Doctor of Medicine and Master of Surgery of the University of Edinburgh. He graduated in 1873, and became Resident Medical Officer at the City of Edinburgh Workhouse, which appointment he held until the following December, when he was elected as one of the medical officers of Wadsley Asylum. Dr McDowall will enter upon his duties at Menston on the 9th April next, and as the result of his long experience at Wadsley, he will be able to give the committee valuable assistance in preparing the asylum for the reception of patients. In the first instance it is intended to furnish a portion of the buildings so as to provide accomodation for 450 patients. Provision has been made for 1,300.

Friday May 18th 1888

New Lunatic Asylum at Menston

On the 1st of September the new asylum at Menston will be opened for the accomodation of pauper lunatics. This is the third establishment of the kind erected in the West Riding, those at Wakefield and Wadsley

(Sheffield) having been respectively completed for use in 1819 and 1874. The necessity for additional asylum accomodation is not altogether due to the normal increase, but in some measure to a tendency on the part of Boards of Guardians to send patients from workhouses to the asylums. The provision at Wakefield has been utilised to the full for many years, and the Wadsley Asylum has been accordingly called upon to admit those which the establishment at Wakefield could not entertain. Seven years ago, however, it was seen that the demands upon the Wadsley Asylum were so severe that the erection of another institution could no longer be ignored.

The Committee of Justices have at present under consideration the furnishing of Menston Asylum, the Court having at the April sessions ordered them to proceed with the work. It is intended, at present, only to furnish accomodation for 300 patients, some of whom will be drafted from the other asylums, while various adjacent unions will send their imbeciles from time to time. The sections of the institution to be furnished in view of coming requirements will be the main portion of the administrative block, the officers' quarters, the medical superintendent's residence, one junior medical officer's house, the matron's lodgings, both the sick and infirm blocks, and the laundry department and residence. It is anticipated that this provision will be ample for the first twelve months; and that the experience then gained will add to the efficiency of the furnishing appointments to be subsequently carried out. The entire capacity of the new asylum when finally completed will be equal to that of either of the other two county asylums.

To accomodate 1,500 patients, the Menston Asylum will entail an expenditure of no less than £350,000, but having in mind the character of the materials and the somewhat expensive style, it is thought that this property will bear favourable comparison with the other asylums of the Riding. It should be added that there remains to be built at Menston a church for the use of the asylum inmates. While the approximate cost will be £10,000, the amount to be actually spent will rest with the Justices. The edifice is to accomodate 790 persons, and will comprise chancel, nave, aisles, organ-chamber and vestry. The building will be in the Tudor period. The erection of a tower will probably be left to a future date.

The new asylum stands at the foot of Rombald's Moor, upon an estate, bounded on the east by the Kirkstall and Otley road, which was purchased for nearly £18,000 from Mr Ayscough Fawkes, of Farnley Hall. The estate slopes gently from a height of 694 feet to 420 feet above the sea level. The institution is built with a large administrative block in the centre, crowned by a noble clock-tower; and the various departments stand transversely to the wings on either hand. The whole presents a southern elevation of more than three-fifths of a mile in extent. The facade, however, is further relieved by small towers, which rise above the different blocks, and serve for ventilation and other essential purposes. The asylum may therefore be spoken of as an enormous range, rather than as a big pile, of buildings. The adoption of the Domestic Tudor as the style of the structure will give a free circulation of air to every part of the establishment, while the design permits to the largest extent of a practical division of departments, and the admission, either through windows of the ordinary class, or by means of skylights, of an abundance of natural light.

It is clear that to provide an asylum for 1,500 patients is to entail the construction of a considerable edifice. The fact that the work will at the time of opening have required continuous labour for three and a half years; that at times 500 workpeople have been simultaneously employed on the undertaking; that the corridor in the central block is 239 feet long, and that from it range corridors on each hand no less than 420 feet long; and that the buildings and pleasure-grounds have absorbed 24 acres of the estate, will indicate the immensity of the institution which has been placed so conveniently in relation to the populous parts of the Riding, and withal in so happy a situation in respect of health and beauty. The whole of the exterior is in stone from the Horsforth quarries, with pierpoints of stone from Idle. The buildings are plain and substantial in the architectural details, but as seen in the mass from the distance they present an imposing appearance.

THE BUILDINGS

The administrative block in the centre stands at a level of 475 feet above the sea. From the entrance it goes back 409 feet, and altogether embraces more than two acres of ground. The left wing will be occupied by the female patients, and the right by the male patients, and in connection with each there are departments for the sick and infirm, the recent and acute cases, and, at the extreme ends, for the epileptic patients. Wards for chronic patients are also to be erected. The entrance hall to the administrative block is flanked by committee rooms, magistrates' room, residence and offices for the medical superintendent, the matron, medical officers, and assistant medical officers; apartments for the clerk and steward, a library, a surgery and dispensary, and separate waiting rooms for male and female visitors, with entrances from a transverse corridor, into which the entrance hall also opens. The hall is floored in mosaic, with a centre-piece representing the White Rose of York. The magistrates' room is wainscoted in oak, and the windows are enriched with stained glass.

The transverse corridor, communicating with all parts of the block, is lighted from the roof and also from side windows, with Burmantofts architraves and other similar work; while the dado of the entire corridor is in similar faience. Beyond the corridor, to which it gives entrance, is the women's dining hall. This is also fitted up as a recreation room and theatre. The hall is 104 feet long and 50 feet wide, and is fine alike in dimensions and general arrangement. There are dado and frieze in Burmantofts work, string courses, and above these, arched windows, which form a further decorative feature. The windows are filled with cathedral glass, and long sprays of bramble with birds flitting about are painted upon it with charming effect. The ceiling is panelled and covered in light brown and gold, and picked out with various tints, all harmonising with the rich hues of dado and frieze, as well as with a magnificent arcaded gallery in walnut. At the opposite end is a large stage, fitted with all requisites in the shape of wings and flies, and accomodation for the band behind the footlights. The arch of the proscenium is a bold feature, and is done in a flowing foliage pattern with fibrous plaster. In convenient proximity are serving rooms and pantries.

To the west of the recreation room, and on the opposite side of a dividing corridor which runs northwards, is the men's dining hall, 133ft by 40ft in dimensions, with an ante-room at its north end. The dining room is lighted from an area on the west side of the administrative block, the light being admitted by means of a glass and wood framework partition, taking the place of a wall. Two square bays improve the appearance of the room very considerably. Compared to the women's dining hall, the style is much plainer, but it is equally chaste. A classic frieze accords with the general treatment, and enriched trusses support the flat arches of the bays. The dado is in glazed brick, with a brown capital and leaf enrichment.

At the end of the dining hall is a short corridor, in which are bays with large windows, where the inmates may enjoy a lounge or a smoke; while there are ventilators for carrying off the smoke. Further to the rear of the administrative buildings are a kitchen 50ft by 40ft, and a scullery 40ft by 30ft, both 26ft high. These places have open iron skeleton roofs, high dados of glazed bricks with fluted chocolate bands and stone-paved floors. The floor of the scullery is slightly inclined, and deep channels are placed to receive and carry away the water which has been used for domestic purposes. Though the kitchen and scullery are in the centre of the block, they are lighted from large areas on either side.

Further to the north, and in direct communication with the culinary department, are vegetable preparing rooms, meat stores, dairies, and bakehouse and flour store, and every necessary convenience, arranged on the most approved system. These store-rooms at the end of the administrative block overlook a delivery yard, into which there runs a special railway line, three-quarters of a mile long, which has been constructed by the West Riding authorities, and which joins the Midland Railway Company's line about halfway between Menston and Guiseley. The serviceableness of the railway has more than twice convered its cost, and it still remains in use in the conveyance of goods and stores to the asylum, and will be of immense future benefit. Including land, the railway cost about £5,000.

VENTILATION AND SANITARY ARRANGEMENTS

Special care has been taken in connection with the sanitary arrangements of the institution, and, indeed, no pains seem to have been wanting to secure efficiency in this respect. In the first place, no drain of any kind is allowed to pass through the residential buildings. In the rear of each of the buildings, and connected only by short passages, are little blocks which have been fitted up as bathrooms, water-closets and lavatories. Except in cases where the corridors must be intersected, iron pipes with lead joints are used for carrying away waste, and a thorough system of trapping and ventilation, on the most modern method, is brought into use. There are manholes at the intersections of all main drains, and the latter will be periodically flushed and thoroughly cleansed. Roof water and service water will be conveyed along a cutting to a brook which bounds one side of the estate, and other convenient points of discharge. The soil drain is quite separate from the rainfall system. The system of drainage in use is called the straight-line and manhole system, the advantage of which is that if there is a stoppage or a fault of any kind in the drains, it can be seen at a glance from the manhole, and the defect easily remedied.

The whole plan of waste disposal has been designed by Mr Edwards, who has given the subject his special consideration. It is intended to construct a sewage farm, and then the sewage from the whole of the institution will be sent to the farm for filtration prior to finding its outlet in the running streams on the estate. Thorough ventilation of all parts of the buildings is secured by means of upcast shafts, inserted in the walls of the rooms, and carried to a chamber which runs round the roof, and is connected with the ventilating towers. Cold air inlets are provided near to the floor line, but the temperature of the incoming air is made more satisfactory by means of hot-water coils. Open fireplaces, mostly on the Teale principle, are provided in the larger rooms and these are supplemented by hot-water coils, which will supply ample warmth. The administrative block, the laundry, and the laundry residence, however, depend for heat entirely on steam coils.

Every necessary precaution against fire has been taken. Fire hydrants in considerable numbers are distributed throughout the buildings, there are fireproof ceilings between the ground floors and the first floors of the blocks, and as soon as occupation commences a fire engine and the best fire extinguishing apparatus will be placed in the building which has been erected for the purpose. A plentiful supply of water for all purposes is obtainable. A spring at High Royds will yield 160,000 gallons per day of water, which has been analysed by Mr Allen, the county analyst, and found to be exceptionally pure and well adapted for domestic purposes. The county authority have constructed at an altitude of 700ft, a reservoir capable of holding a three months' supply, calculated on an estimated rate of consumption. The lighting of the building is intended to be mainly by gas, but to some small extent Wenham lamps will be used. The supply of gas will be obtained from the Yeadon Gasworks. The Justices have on several occasions discussed the question of electric lighting, but cost, and probably improvements in the future, have induced them to defer the adoption of this light until they are warranted from economical and other points of view in substituting it for illumination by means of gas.

The whole of the work connected with the building and arrangement of the new asylum has been carried out from the designs of Mr Edwards, the county surveyor; and it will stand as a monument to his energy and skill. It is believed that when finished the establishment will be as complete in all its details as any similar institution in the country. Messrs Whitaker Bros., of Horsforth, are the contractors for the whole of the building operations. Mr Henry Webb has been clerk of the works in the case of this important undertaking.

Amongst the most important sub-contractors are the following: Gasfittings, Milnes, Son and Mcfie, of Edinburgh; stained glass, Messrs Campbell and Smith of London; electrical arrangements, Messrs Adams and Co of London; lightning conductors, Messrs Berry and Sons of Huddersfield; mosaic work, Messrs O'Neill and Co., of Liverpool; slating and plastering, Messrs Rushworth and Firth, of Halifax; bakers' ovens, Mr W. F. Mason of Manchester; porcelain baths, Messrs Joseph Cliff and Sons; vanes and finials, Messrs Hart, Son, Peard and Co; slate, the Buttermere Green Slate Company, Keswick; joiners' work (with the exception of special contracts) Messrs Taylor Bros., of Yeadon; patent locks, Messrs Kaye and Sons of Leeds and London; heating apparatus, Messrs Haden and Sons, of Trowbridge; sanitary arrangements, Mr Clark, of Wolverhampton, and Messrs Sharp Bros of Burton-on-Trent; Stamford joint piping, Messrs Ingham and Sons, Wortley; painting and decorating, Mr E. Harland, Manor Row, Bradford; the clock in the tower, Messrs Potts and Sons, of Leeds; plumbing and glazing, Mr Braithwaite, of Leeds; fittings in the recreation hall, Messrs Marsh, Jones and Cribb, of Leeds; and ventilators, Messrs Kershaw of Lancaster.

December 21st 1888.

Report of part of a speech made by Mr Francis Darwin at a political meeting of electors, Victoria Hall, Ilkley.

(Mr Darwin said:) 'The charge which was distinctly made was that in the purchase of the (Menston Asylum) estate, too much had been paid for it. Now he would tell the whole story of the matter. The estate was purchased of Mr A. Fawkes. It consisted of 283 acres; £17,000 was paid for it. In 1877, he himself (viz Darwin), as a private individual, had negotiated for that very estate. He offered £15,000 for it, and Mr Fawkes declined it, and said he would take not less than £17,000. When they had to build an asylum, the magistrates were told that there were three things primarily essential. One was proximity to Bradford, which was a large and important town; the same consideration was required for Leeds; and also easy access from the northern portion of the Riding, from which it was supposed the chief number of the patients would come, the patients from the other parts going to Wadsley and Wakefield.

'It struck him (Darwin) that the Menston site possessed these essentials and he asked Lord Wharncliffe, Mr Aldam, Mr Stanhope, and some other gentlemen to meet him on the spot and inspect the site, and without any hesitation they all said there could not be a better site. He, (Darwin) at their request, approached Mr Fawkes. When they had to purchase land for a particular purpose it was not wise to hesitate lest their particular purpose might become known to the seller. He saw Mr Fawkes, who offered to sell the land for £17,000, and he closed with the offer. The land cost £60 per acre, and he had no hesitation in saying – without any egotism – that that purchase saved the West Riding at least £10,000.' (Applause).

Appendix 7:

The Hawksworth Estate situate in the West Riding of the County of York belonging to F. H. Fawkes Esqr of Farnley Hall, Otley.

Report of Hollis and Webb, Estate Auctioneers and Surveyors, May 1900.

We have made an inspection of this Estate for the purpose of forming an opinion of its value and of advising as to what we consider is necessary in arranging for an early realisation.

The total area of the Estate is upwards of 2,300 acres and it may be described as being within a ring fence. The land varies greatly in quality ranging from fairly good agricultural and accomodation land to strong coarse soil and moorland. We attach much importance to its situation as it is in the heart of the Great Industrial Centres of the West Riding of Yorkshire, near to Leeds, Bradford, Shipley, Bingley and other manufacturing Towns and therefore most favourably placed for obtaining unlimited quantities of tillage and for the sale of produce direct to the consumer.

The agricultural part of the Estate is divided into a number of small holdings varying from 23 acres to 195 acres which are occupied principally as milk farms and are in possession of reliable and respectable tenants several of whom and their fathers before them have been on the Estate for long periods. The present rents appear to us to be very moderate and we think they should be well maintained. The population of the neighbouring towns and villages is rapidly increasing and the demand for milk and other farm produce should become greater in consequence. The various homesteads are conveniently placed, but in many cases the buildings are old and dilapidated and the sanitary arrangements and mistal accomodation are far from satisfactory and serious outlay will probably have to be incurred before long as modern legislation is tending towards drastic reform in the drainage and provision of buildings for the housing of cattle on dairy and milk farms, particularly as regards those situated near to large towns. When the reconstruction of Buildings and drains takes place on these farms some increase of rents may be obtained but it is doubtful whether it will be possible to obtain such advances as will be an adequate return on the full amount of capital it will be necessary to expend. The farms are very well watered, but in many parts drainage is much needed.

The Village of Hawksworth is attractively situated in a healthy position. It consists principally of homesteads belonging to the farms and a few cottages and dwelling houses with their gardens. We strongly recommend the expenditure of at least £500 in pointing and repairing many of the buildings and this work should be done at once as the improved appearance of the village might affect the selling value of the Estate to a greater amount than the actual outlay on the repairs. Our attention has been directed to the want of an approach to the Estate on the South Easterly side from the Shipley Road. If a right of road could be obtained it would be a distinct advantage as it would very materially shorten the distance from Lunds Farm to Shipley and Bradford. If possible an option should be obtained by the present owner of Hawksworth at a fixed price, from the owners of the Lands intervening between Lunds Farm and the Shipley Road near Tong Park Mills either of the lands themselves or of a right of road of sufficient width over them, such option to extend beyond the time of the proposed sale of the Hawksworth Estate. This would enable a purchaser to decide for himself as to the question of approach without putting the present Owner of Hawksworth to any additional cost. We may add that whilst an approach to the Estate at this point might be a great convenience to the tenant of Lunds Farm, we do not consider that it would create a demand for any of the Hawksworth Land for building purposes. In our opinion, this immediate locality is not yet ripe for building development.

Hawksworth Hall with its pleasure grounds, Plantation, Gardens, Outbuildings and enclosures and Land is let on lease until May 1st 1914 to Duncan George Law Esqr, the rent to May 1st 1901 being £75, from 1901 to 1906 £90, and from 1906 to 1914 £125. When inspecting the Hall and premises we noticed that the Lessee was making alterations and improvements on a very extensive scale, and as a result this portion of the Estate should revert to the owners at the termination of the Lease, greatly enhanced in value. In the meantime the existence of the lease prevents anyone but the lessee from occupying the Mansion. Possibly this fact together with the Hall Croft being occupied also on Lease by the Bradford Golf Club, may to some slight extent be prejudicial to the Sale, as the Mansion may naturally be considered the Residence of the owner of the Estate. On the other hand so seriously dilapidated had it become that, had it not been let on lease it would have been necessary to expend quite £2000 on repairs and alterations in order to have rendered it suitable for either the Owner or an ordinary yearly tenant.

The Woods and Plantations cover an area of about 70 acres. Although there are many well grown trees, much of the timber is small and we attach more importance to it as offering excellent cover for game forming shelters, and from an ornamental point of view, than to its value as timber. There are indications of the existence of a quantity of stone on the

Estate, as is testified by the disused quarries and by the quarry which is being worked on Reva Side Farm; but we do not consider that this materially enhances the value of the Estate, because of the distance of the quarries from the Railway.

The Sporting Advantages (apart from those of the Moor which will be referred to hereafter) are fairly good, the Estate is well stocked with game and no doubt excellent sport may be had by a sporting man, who like the present tenant Mr T. M. Holmes maintains friendly relations with the tenant farmers and strictly preserves. The advantage of having a good shooting almost within half an hour of their homes or places of business must be a strong inducement to many businessmen in the neighbouring towns.

The Golf Links: So long as Golf maintains its popularity these links will be attractive, at present they are held under lease by the Bradford Golf Club at an annual rental of £184 16s 0d for a term of 20 years from January 1899. In this case the land should revert to the Owners of the Estate at the termination of the lease improved in quality. If Golf continues to be popular the renewal of the present lease at an increased rental should easily be arranged as the links should be much more suitable for the game at the end than at the beginning of the first 20 years. It will be seen therefore that the Lands occupied as the Golf links should, whether retained or abandoned by the Club, increase in value.

Hawksworth moor an area of about 580 acres adjoins Burley Moor, the property of Mrs Crofton, and for many years the latter had been held under lease-hold tenure by the Owner of Hawksworth Moor, the two covering about 2,000 acres, being retained by him or let for sporting purposes. They are well stocked with grouse and being within three miles of several Railway Stations their sporting advantage should command a high rental. The existing lease of Burley Moor was granted to the Rev. F. Fawkes from June 21st 1899 for a term of 5 years at a yearly rental of £125, and last year the two moors were let together by Mr Fawkes for £300. In view of the sale of this Estate, we should advise that an extension of the lease be if possible obtained from Mrs Crofton, of Burley Moor, say for ten or fifteen years, as we are of opinion that the acquisition of the sporting right over 2,000 acres of good Grouse Moors for fifteen or twenty years would add considerably to the general desirability of the Estate. Water rights on Hawksworth Moor have been acquired by absolute purchase by the Yeadon Waterworks Co and the Baildon Urban District Council.

The Rifle Range on Hawksworth Moor has been let hitherto on yearly tenancy for a mere acknowledgement for use by the Burley Company of the 3rd Vol: Battalion Duke of Wellington's (W.R.) Regiment, but an intending purchaser would be justified in considering it a source of income. The conditions of modern warfare have brought Rifle ranges into extra-ordinary prominence and importance and the difficulties in the way of obtaining long ranges within reasonable distances of large towns are being severely felt and are adding greatly to the value of existing ranges. We are of opinion that this range should be worth a rental of £100 per annum.

Outgoings: There is an annual Tithe rent charge of £66 1s 6d which belongs in equal moieties to the Owner of Hawksworth and Messrs Ray and Fitzroy. This must therefore be treated as a deduction from the rents of £33 0s 9d as the holdings are let tithe free. We are not aware of any other outgoings beyond repairs, management, and the cost of preserving Hawksworth Moor. The repairs are likely to be a serious item because of the dilapidated condition of many of the buildings.

In conclusion we recommend that the Estate be offered for sale by public auction in its entirety. It is so compact and possesses as a whole advantages and points of interest which would be sacrificed if it were broken up into lots. We cannot but think that so fine an Estate offered by auction would attract the attention and competition of the wealthier capitalists of the West Riding and it would not surprise us if the price realised, considerably exceeded the figure we should recommend as a reserve viz:– Sixty Thousand Pounds £60,000.

This figure we have arrived at after making a most careful valuation and after having given full consideration to all the various points which have suggested themselves to us. No time should be lost, trade is good, the Estate market is brisk, money is still cheap, in short conditions generally are favourable to realisation.

May 8th 1900 Hollis & Webb

Author's footnote: Shortly after this report was submitted, steps were taken to prepare for an auction of the whole of the Hawksworth Estate in the manner suggested by Hollis and Webb, and an auctioneer's plan was printed and possibly distributed. However, for some reason Mr F H Fawkes decided not to proceed. The estate was not sold until the summer of 1919. At an auction on the 28th July 1919 the Hawksworth property came under the hammer in twenty separate lots. The sale raised only £17,500. Before the auction sale, Hawksworth Hall had been purchased privately by the sitting tenant, Mr D G Law, for £9,000; and at approximately the same time, three farms – Norcroft, Odda and Thorpe – were sold to High Royds Hospital (West Riding County Council) for £12,500.

Appendix 8:

Yorkshire Evening Post, Tuesday the 29th July 1919

'Land At Less Than A Penny A Yard'

'Hawksworth Estate Sale'

Land at less than 1d per yard, with a farmhouse and outbuildings thrown in! How do prospective West Riding builders regard such a figure, which was the price at which some land changed hands yesterday within a radius of 10 miles of Leeds Town Hall and within five of Bradford? The farm was one of a number of others on the Hawksworth Estate of Mr F. H. Fawkes, of Farnley Hall, near Otley, who offered for sale by auction, through Messrs Dacre and Son, of Otley, practically the whole of his holdings at Hawksworth, near Guiseley, retaining only the golf links, which are let on lease to the Bradford Golf Club.

The lot which went for this low figure is Intake Farm, which consists of a farmhouse, barn, stabling for four horses, mistal for 24 cattle, cart shed, and other buildings and 100 acres of land. It was bought by Mr F. J. Riddihough for £1,600, which is £16 an acre, or just over ³⁄₄d per yard. There are plenty of allotment holders paying ½d per yard rent for their plots. How would they like to buy the land on a two years' purchase?

Although this was the cheapest lot in the sale there were several others of interest. One of these was a plot of 2,510 yards of land, which was bought by Mr Walter Breary for £100, or about 10d per yard. Even this should be cheap enough for a man who wants to build a house in the country. Lane Side Farm, occupying 129 acres, and let to Mr Arthur Gill at a rental of £198 with a tithe rent charge of £9 6s 2d was bought by Ald. Richard Garnett, acting on behalf of the West Riding County Council, for £5,000.

Sunnyside Farm, of 103 acres, was bought by Mr F. Towler for £2,700 and Sunny Vale Farm by Mr Richard Denton for £950. Storth House Farm, of 150 acres, went to Mr F. J. Riddihough, for £2,500, and Mr J. W. Padgett of Rawdon, bought Hill Side Farm, of 35 acres, for £1,050. Mr S. J. Wood, of Otley, was the purchaser of Brown Cow House and 3 acres, 3 roods of land for £650, and Spring Side farm and five dwelling houses, with 10 acres, 3 roods, 25 perches of land was bought by the tenant of the farm, Mr T. A. Atkinson, for £1,200.

The Hawksworth Schoolhouse and garden went to Mr F. Davey for £410, a cottage and garden was purchased by Mrs Webb for £260, and two other cottages by Mr Hullah for £535. A plot of building land at the foot of Hollings Hill, 1 acre, 24 perches in extent, was bought by Messrs Denby, of Tong Park, for £100. Some interest was taken in the sale of Windyridge cottage, made prominent by Mr W. Riley, the novelist. It is a one-storey building, and was sold for £400 to Mrs Clarke, who also bought 1 acre, 2 roods, 14 perches of building land for £80.

Many of the larger lots were withdrawn, as the amount offered was below the reserve price. These included Thorpe Farm, 60 acres, withdrawn at £2,000; Hall Croft Farm, in the middle of the village, 65 acres, £2,400; Lund's Farm, 126 acres, £2,300; Intake Farm, 87½ acres, £2,500; Hawksworth Mill Farm, 105 acres, £2,400. Lane Side cottage was not offered. Prior to the sale, Hawksworth Hall, the residence of Mr Duncan G. Law, was purchased privately by the tenant, and also a plot of ground by the West Riding County Council for the extension of Menston Asylum.

Outline pedigree showing links between Ayscough, Hawksworth, Fawkes and Ramsden families in the eighteenth century

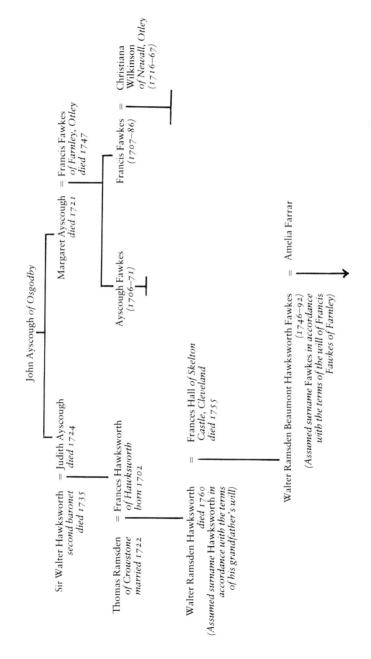

Outline pedigree showing the links between the Breary, Beckwith, Fairfax, Rhodes, Fourness and Pulleyn families in the seventeenth and eighteenth centuries

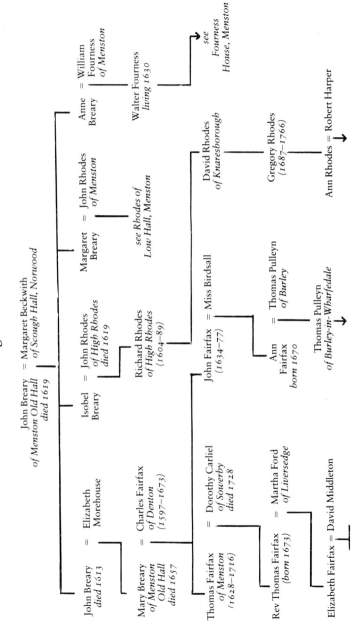

Outline pedigree of the Rhodes of Low Hall, Menston

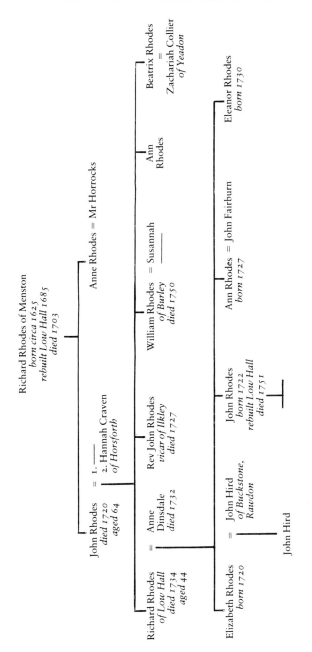

The Rules, Orders, And Regulations Of The London Cemetery Company

The Rules, Orders, and Regulations

OF THE

LONDON CEMETERY COMPANY.

(*Incorporated by Act of Parliament.*)

Cemeteries.

ST. JAMES, AT HIGHGATE;

F. W. TA' BOIS, *Superintendent.*

ALL SAINTS, AT NUNHEAD, PECKHAM RYE;

E. MARTIN, *Superintendent.*

OFFICES:

Chief—29, NEW BRIDGE ST., BLACKFRIARS,

AND AT THE CEMETERIES.

W. WALTON,

Secretary.

FEBRUARY 7th, 1878.

THE

RULES, ORDERS, AND REGULATIONS

OF THE

LONDON CEMETERY COMPANY,

Made pursuant to 6 & 7 William, cap. cxxxvi., and 6 Victoria,
cap. xxxvi.,

*For the Management and Regulation of their Cemeteries,
and of the Catacombs, Vaults, Graves, and
Monuments therein.*

———

February 7th, 1878.

Relating to Grave Owners and Undertakers:

(1.)—Thirty-six hours' notice shall be given before interments. If an interment be appointed for a Monday, notice shall be given not later than on the preceding Friday. Four clear days' notice shall be given if a Vault or Brick Grave be required. If the requisite notice be not given, an extra charge for working at night shall be paid before the ground is opened.

(2.)—The price to be paid for the grant of an exclusive right of burial, and all fees and charges, shall be in accordance with Schedule A, and must be paid at the Office or at the Cemetery when the order is given, and the full name, age, and place of abode of the deceased, the size of coffin, and the name and address of the undertaker, must be stated at the same time.

(3.)—No order shall be taken for an interment including the purchase of a new Grave unless the name and address of the person to be registered as owner be supplied at the time, or, in exceptional cases, the name of the person by whom the undertaker is employed.

(4.)—No Catacomb, Vault, or Grave in which the exclusive right of burial has been purchased, shall be opened without the owner's consent in writing, which is to be lodged at the time the order is given.

(5.)—The name of the parish or ecclesiastical district from which the body is to be removed shall be stated at the time of paying the dues.

(6.)—The Funeral Service will be performed by the Company's Chaplain in the consecrated portion of the Cemetery. A Dissenting Minister will be provided for funerals in the unconsecrated portion. The friends of the deceased may, if they prefer it, provide the Minister in either case, 24 hours' notice being given in writing of their desire so to do, either at the Office or at the Cemetery.

(7.)—All Vaults or Brick Graves shall be opened from the top, unless by special permission.

(8.)—No interment shall be made in a Catacomb, Vault, or Brick Grave, unless the coffin be of lead, stone, or asphalte.

(9.)—In Common Graves coffins of wood only shall be used, and no Monument or Grave-stone will be allowed.

(10.)—All brickwork and masonry to Vaults, Graves, and Foundations, and all Facings or Tablets to Catacomb Chambers and Compartments, with the inscriptions thereon, shall be executed by the Company, and shall be paid for as per Schedule B.

(11.)—A Monument or Grave-stone, first approved by the Directors, shall be erected within 12 months from the date of the first interment in any Grave in which the exclusive right of burial has been purchased, otherwise the right shall be forfeited.

(12.)—Every Monument, Grave-stone, or other erection, shall be maintained in good order and condition by the owner thereof, otherwise the right of burial shall be forfeited.

(13.)—The Company's charges for executing gardeners' work upon the surface of the Graves in the Cemeteries shall be as per Schedule C; all Grave owners desirous of turfing, planting, or otherwise ornamenting their Graves themselves, must make application to the Superintendent at the Cemetery or to the Directors.

(14.)—Where exclusive right of burial has been purchased either in a Grave or Vault within 20 feet of any road, a Monument must be erected; but in remoter distances Grave-stones will be allowed.

(15.)—Before the erection of any Monument or Grave-stone, a drawing thereof, with the proposed inscription, shall be submitted for approval, and deposited in the Superintendent's office at the Cemetery, accompanied by a "Mason's order," signed by the owner of the Grave.

(16.)—No Mason or other person will be allowed to execute work in the Cemetery without first lodging the authority of the owner of the Grave with the Superintendent, and obtaining his "permit."

(17.)—Cramps of copper only shall be used in the erection of Tablets or Monuments.

(18.)—Before erecting a Tomb or Monument over an earth Grave, the Grave shall be covered with a hard York landing not less than four inches thick as a foundation; and the Tomb or Monument, with the said landing, shall not exceed one ton in weight.

(19.)—A stone kerb, intended to support a ledger stone or an iron railing, or used merely as a border upon a Grave not larger than 6 ft. 6 in. by 5 ft. 4 in., shall not be less than 5 in. thick by 8 in. deep, or upon a larger Grave shall not be less than 6 in. thick by 8 in. deep, and shall rest upon three transverse pieces of hard Yorkshire stone, each piece being not less than 9 in. broad and 3 in. thick, but on all Graves stone kerbs fixed on landings may be not less than 4 in. in thickness where no posts or standards of any kind are inserted; not less than 5 in. in case of any insertion. Marble kerbs on landings may be not less than 4 in. in either case. Each side kerb must be in one piece, except where fixed on a landing with posts of larger dimensions.

(20.)—No Bath, Caen, or other soft stone will be allowed in the erection of any Monument or Gravestone.

(21.)—All persons working within the Cemetery shall conform in all respects to the Rules, Orders, and Regulations in force for the conduct of the business of the Cemetery, and shall be subject to the control of the Superintendent.

(22.)—All masons and other persons having work within the Cemetery shall, on each occasion of their admission, enter their names and those of their employers at the Superintendent's Office, and shall make a deposit of 10s., which will be repaid upon their clearing up all dirt and rubbish, and on leaving, provided they shall have conformed to all the Company's Rules, Orders, and Regulations; but in default thereof, or in case of damage occasioned wilfully, or by reason of negligence in workmanship, or otherwise, the deposit shall be forfeited to the Company, and such forfeiture shall be without prejudice to any other remedy the Company may have.

(23.)—All workmen and other persons failing to conform to any of the Rules, Orders, and Regulations, or misbehaving themselves, or speaking with incivility to Visitors or to any of the Officers of the Company, shall immediately be removed from the Cemetery.

(24.)—Any person soliciting orders within the Cemetery for the erection or repair of Monuments and Tombstones, for the flowering or turfing of Graves, or for any other work connected with the Graves, shall be removed from the Cemetery, and shall not again be admitted within the Company's premises.

(25.)—No workmen or materials shall be admitted within the Cemetery before six o'clock in the morning between Lady Day and Michaelmas; or before half-past eight o'clock between Michaelmas and Lady Day; or after four o'clock p.m.; or on Saturdays after twelve o'clock at noon.

(26.)—No workmen shall remain in the Cemetery in the evening after the time specified by the Superintendent.

(27.)—Works of every description shall be carried on continuously, and be completed with all reasonable expedition; on default, the Superintendent's "Permit" will be void.

(28.)—No Carts or Trucks of any description shall remain in the Cemetery longer than is necessary for unloading or loading, nor shall they be turned on the road or turf.

(29.)—Smoking is strictly prohibited within the Cemetery.

(30.)—No dog shall be admitted on any consideration.

(31.)—Visitors are on no account to pluck the flowers or shrubs, to sit on the tombs, railings, or slopes, or to walk across the grass.

(32.)—All perambulators, baskets, parcels, bags, and flowers must be left with the Gatekeeper during the time that the owners thereof remain in the Cemetery.

(33.)—No carriage shall be admitted into the Cemetery without special permission, unless in attendance upon a Funeral.

(34.)—Subject to the Rules, Orders, and Regulations of the Company, the Public will be allowed to visit the Cemeteries on every week day from 9 a.m. till the ringing of the bell in the evening at the hour to be daily posted at the gates. On Sundays, Christmas Day, and Good Friday the Cemeteries will be open only from 1 to 4 p.m. from October to March inclusive, and from 2 to 6 p.m. from April to September inclusive. No business shall be done on those days.

(35.)—All persons admitted into the Cemetery shall be subject to the orders and control of the Superintendent and the Officers of the Company.

Schedules hereinbefore referred to, viz.:—

SCHEDULE A.

CHARGES to be made on the sale of the exclusive right of Burial or Interment in perpetuity in any Catacomb, Brick Grave, Earth Grave, or other place of Burial as enumerated below, or as may be arranged upon the prices set forth, viz. :—

HIGHGATE CEMETERY.

Lebanon Catacomb Chamber, fitted complete.
    with shelves for 15 coffins ...   ... from 200 guineas.
Avenue Catacomb Chamber, fitted with
    shelves for 12 coffins ...   . ,, 130 ,,
Terrace Catacomb Chamber, fitted with
    shelves and iron door ...   . ,, 220 ,,
  Marble or stone facings according to arrangement.
Terrace Catacomb Compartment—

for 1 coffin, from £10	10 to	£15	15
,, 2 ,, ,, 20	0 to	30	0
,, 3 ,, ,, 30	0 to	45	0
,, 4 ,, ,, 38	0 to	58	0

Other Catacomb Chambers for Families according
    to situation ...   . from £110

NUNHEAD CEMETERY.

Chapel Catacombs—

for 1 coffin £15	15	0
,, 2 ditto 30	0	0
,, 2 ditto in Central Compartments, including marble tablet, from £35 to 36	15	0
,, 3 coffins 45	0	0
,, 4 ditto 60	0	0

Eastern Catacombs, for each coffin £10 10 0

Shaft ditto ditto 4 4 0

Ground for Construction of—

    Brick Grave, for 12 coffins, size 9 ft.

        0 in. by 6 ft. 6 in. ... ...£21 0 0 to 31 10 0

    Step entrance to the same, size 6 ft.

        6 in. by 5 ft. 0 in.... ... ... 21 0 0

Where step entrance is built in the roadway, the ground is not

        sold, and the brickwork must be built in cement.

    Brick Grave, for 6 coffins, size 9 ft.

        0 in. by 4 ft. 0 in.... ... ...£15 15 0 to 21 0 0

Private Grave, not to be bricked,

    size 9 ft. 0 in. by 6 ft. 6 in. ... 21 0 0 to 31 10 0

Private Grave, not to be bricked,

    size 9 ft. 0 in. by 4 ft. 0 in. ... 15 15 0 to 21 0 0

Private Grave, not to be bricked,

    size 6 ft. 6 in. by 2 ft. 10 in. ... 4 9 0 to 6 6 0

Private Grave, not to be bricked,

    size 6 ft. 6 in. by 2 ft. 6 in. ... 3 3 0 to 5 5 0

7 feet deep.

In select spots ground for Mausoleum, Family Grave

    with step entrance, brick or earth grave, or as

    extra ground attached to any such grave—

        per superficial foot, according to position, 10s. to 25s.

The Charge for Single Deposit—

    In the public vault shall be £5 5 0

    In a catacomb compartment for a term not ex-

        ceeding twelve months 5 5 0

    In a common grave, including use of chapel and

        service, at 10 a.m. and 3 p.m. only—

            Each adult 2 2 0

            Each child under 8 years ... 1 10 0

The Charge for Excavating in all ground shall be—

    For extra depth, and reopening a private grave

        beyond 7 ft. to

            8 ft. £0 2 6 ... 11 ft. £0 10 6

            9 ,, 0 5 0 ... 12 ,, 0 13 6

            10 ,, 0 7 6 ... 13 ,, 0 16 6

For extra depth, and re-opening a private grave
beyond 7 ft. to

14 ft.	£0	19	6	...	20 ft.	£1	19	6
15 ,,	1	2	6	...	21 ,,	2	4	6
16 ,,	1	5	6	...	22 ,,	2	9	6
17 ,,	1	9	0	...	23 ,,	2	14	6
18 ,,	1	12	6	...	24 ,,	2	19	6
19 ,,	1	16	0	...	25 ,,	3	4	6

Beyond 25 ft., 7s. 6d. per foot.

Excavating for Mausoleums, Foundations, and Brick Graves,
3s. 6d. per cubic yard.

The Charge for Fees on Interment to be paid, in addition to
the charges for the purchase of any Catacomb or Ground on
each occasion of interment therein, shall be—

	Each Adult.	Each child under 8 years.
In Mausoleums and Private Graves, with extra ground	£6 6 0	£4 4 0
,, Catacomb		
,, Private Vault or Brick Grave ...		
,, ground for Brick Grave or Private Grave on the Terrace, Highgate, or other spaces in either Cemetery, as per agreement ...	5 5 0	3 10 0
,, Private Grave, 6 ft. 6 in. by 2 ft. 6 in. or 2 ft. 10 in. ...	2 2 0	1 8 0
,, Ditto ditto, in select places	3 3 0	2 2 0
,, Public Vault	5 5 0	3 10 0

On removal from or to other places of Interment—

	Each Body.
To Catacomb	
,, Private Vault or Brick Grave	£2 2 0
,, Earth Grave 9 ft. by 4 ft., or 9 ft. by 6 ft. 6 in.	
,, Private Grave, 6 ft. 6 in. by 2 ft. 6 in. or 2 ft. 10 in.	1 1 0
,, Public Vault	2 2 0
From any Grave	1 1 0

Other charges, not specified in the foregoing, shall be as follows, viz. :—

	£	s	d
On all interments before 2 o'clock, or at and after 5 p.m. during the summer, or sunset during winter	0	7	6
Use of large Weather Screen	0	5	0
Interment of a still-born child	0	5	0
„ of an unbaptised child not more than seven days old	0	5	0
Ditto ditto in a Private Grave, 2s. per foot excavating from surface, and fee ...	0	10	0
Entry of grant	0	2	6
Stamp duty on grant	*Ad valorem*		
Certificate of Burial and Search	0	3	7
Comparing and Searching Register, for one year	0	1	0
„ „ „ for every additional year	0	0	6
Space for a Monumental Tablet or Brass inside Chapel, or on outside of Colonnade Walls, per foot superficial at from	10/6 to 21/-		
Opening and reclosing Mausoleum, Brick Grave, Catacomb Chamber, or Compartment	1	1	0
Opening and reclosing Brick Grave with step entrance	2	2	0
Turfing a Grave	0	2	6
Removing and replacing Monuments and Grave Stones, according to assessed charge in the Monumental Books of the Company...			

The Company undertakes by sealed deed, to maintain Graves, and the monuments thereon in perpetuity, upon payment of a sum to be ascertained upon application to the Secretary.

SCHEDULE B.

CHARGES to be made on brickwork and masonry to be executed by the Company, viz. :

	£	s.	d.
For the construction of a Brick Grave, including a 4-inch York Landing, 9 ft. by 6 ft. 6 in. by 10 ft. deep in cement	£32	10	0
,, Ditto ditto in mortar	26	10	0
,, the construction of a Step Entrance, with stone door and cover, 5 ft. by 6 ft. 6 in. in cement	21	0	0
,, Ditto ditto in mortar	17	0	0
,, the construction of Brick Grave, with 4-inch York Landing, 9 ft. by 4 ft. by 10 ft. deep in cement	25	0	0
,, Ditto ditto in mortar	21	0	0
,, Rubbing Landing, face and edges— 9 ft. by 6 ft. 6 in.	2	2	0
,, Ditto ditto 9 ft. by 4 ft.	1	10	0
,, Cutting Landing and raising on Brick Grave 9 ft. by 6 ft. 6 in.	1	12	0
,, Ditto ditto 9 ft. by 4 ft.	1	1	0
,, Cutting Landing, fixed level on Brick Grave 9 ft. by 6 ft. 6 in.	1	1	0
,, Ditto ditto 9 ft. by 4 ft.	0	16	0
,, Iron Bearers for Coffin in Brick Grave— 9 ft. by 6 ft. 6 in.	1	1	0
,, Ditto ditto 9 ft. by 4 ft.	0	15	0
,, Stone Partition in Brick Grave— 9 ft. by 6 ft. 6 in.	3	3	0
,, Ditto ditto 9 ft. by 4 ft.	2	2	0
,, Stone Facings, averaging 15 in. above level of ground, to B. G. 9 ft. by 6 ft. 6 in.	5	5	0

For Stone Facings, averaging 15 in. above level
    of ground to B. G. 9 ft. by 4 ft.   ... £4 4 0
,, Stone Coffin in Earth Grave 5 5 0
,, Marble Tablet for single Catacomb Com-
    partment 1 15 0
,,   Ditto   for double ditto 3 10 0
,, Plate Glass Tablet, for single Catacomb
    Compartment 2 5 0
,, Marble Tablet with plate glass centre
    for ditto 3 0 0
,, Plate Glass Tablet, or Marble Tablet, or
    Marble Table, with plate glass centre,
    in oak frame, with brass lock and hinges
    for single Catacomb Compartment   ... 4 4 0
,, Inscriptions :—
        On Marble Tablets in Catacomb
            Compartments—
                Cutting and blacking, per letter 0 0 2½
                In lead letters, per letter   ... 0 0 6
      On Monuments and Grave Stones
          As may be required per letter from 1½d. to 2 6
,, Repairs to Monuments and Grave Stones as may be
    required, estimate to be obtained from the Superin-
    tendent.
,, All foundations for Mausoleums, Monuments, or other-
    wise, and for the construction of Brick Graves of
    larger dimensions than specified, also for stone or
    marble facings other than specified, as per estimate to
    be obtained from the Superintendent.

SCHEDULE C.

THE Company's charges for gardening shall be as follows, viz. :—

For maintaining with flowers and shrubs according to season, all the year round—

			£	s.	d.
For a Grave, 6½ ft. by 2½ ft. ...	per annum	£1	1	0
,, 6½ ft. by 2 ft. 10 in.	,,	1	1	0
,, 9 ft. by 4 ft. ...	,,	2	2	0
,, 9 ft. by 6 ft. 6 in. ...	,,	3	3	0

Carpet bedding, or any special work at an extra charge, by arrangement with the Superintendent.

For turfing and maintaining the surface in good and neat order all the year round—

			£	s.	d.
For a Grave, 6½ ft. by 2½ ft. ...	per annum	£0	7	6
,, 6½ ft. by 2 ft. 10 in.	,,	0	7	6
,, 9 ft. by 4 ft. ...	,,	0	15	0
,, 9 ft. by 6 ft. 6 in. ...	,,	1	1	0

For turfing once only—

			£	s.	d.
For a Grave, 6½ ft. by 2½ ft. ...	... ...	£0	2	6
,, 6½ ft. by 2 ft. 10 in.	... ...	0	2	6
,, 9 ft. by 4 ft. ...	... ...	0	5	0
,, 9 ft. by 6 ft. 6 in. ...	... ...	0	7	6

Special sizes as required, and according to area to be dealt with.

Plants, shrubs, &c., kept on the premises for selection, and sold separately, when desired.

The Company undertakes, by sealed deed, to maintain the decoration of graves in perpetuity, upon payment of a sum to be ascertained upon application to the Secretary.

By order,

W. WALTON,

FEBRUARY 7th, 1878.   *Secretary.*

N.B.—With reference to Regulations 4, 15, and 16 :—upon the death of the owner of any Grave, it is advisable that the executor or next-of-kin to the deceased do call at the Chief Office as soon as convenient after the interment, and, by production of probate or (in case of intestacy) by declaration of heirship, cause the alteration in ownership to be duly recorded in the Company's Register of Vaults and Graves.

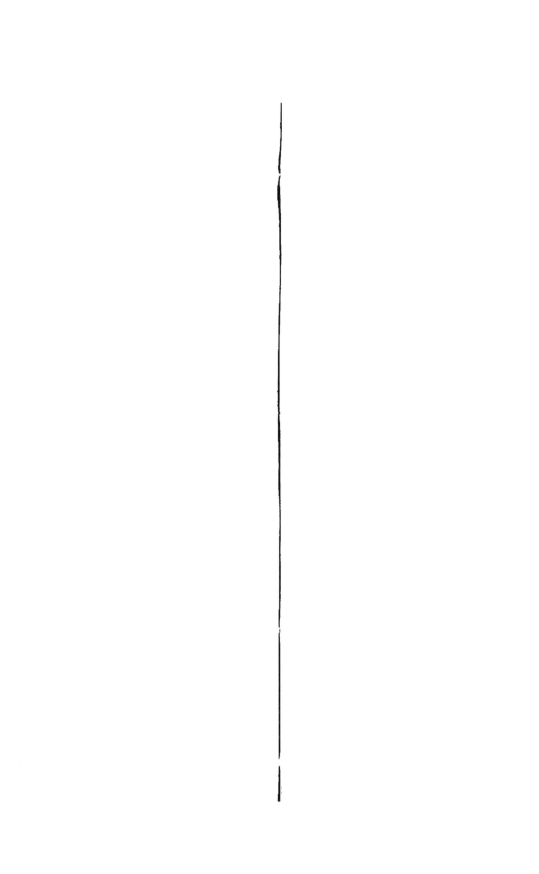